Trained Dogs Don't Bite Children

By Deirdre Ryan

Acknowledgments

I would like to thank my two children Natalie and Stella for giving me the magical gift of being mother.

Thank you to the thousand plus rescue dogs, my own dogs - past and present and clients' dogs who I've learnt from over the last 20 years.

Thank you, John Rogerson, for inspiring my journey to be a dog trainer many years ago and giving me the confidence to pursue my dream.

And thank you to all my friends and family who have supported both my journey to being a mother and an author.

About the Author

Deirdre is a certified dog groomer, dog trainer and behaviourist with 20 years' experience. She competes successfully in many dog sports and lives in Co. Clare, Ireland with her 9-year-old twin Daughters Stella and Natalie, 5 dogs, 3 cats and a hamster.

Find out more at drdogcare.ie

Prologue:

As a single mother, by choice, of twin girls (now aged 9 years) and with little experience of babies, the advice of a good book seemed a sensible option I felt I had a good handle on my 3 dogs behaviour and training, but had no idea if this would transmit to children. Thankfully it did, and I found validation for this through a best-selling parenting book "French Children Don't Throw Food" by Pamela Druckerman.

My routine with my dogs contained a few enforced rules combined with a lot of freedom and self-expression for both them and me.. And it turned out that was exactly what children needed too!

Both my dogs and my children get large doses of love, cuddles, exercise, fun and boundaries. A clear respect and understanding of what they needed. Dogs need love, exercise, freedom of expression and security. Kids - pretty much the same!

So, a few years later when I read an updated version of the aforementioned book, I decided the content and the format merited a doggy version. And so here it is!

I hope it will help your dogs (and your kids) enjoy a full, contented, loving and secure life.

The format of this book is inspired by the parenting methods in "French Parents don't Give In", by Pamela Druckerman. It is 100 concise chapters which covers a diverse number of topics. The first half of the book roughly covers the puppies first 6 months of life. The middle of the book covers more formal training, and the last few chapters cover potential problems and how to solve them.

As the main chapter titles are inspired by the French book, I have included the easier to interpret subtitles below as an easy reference.

1

Getting a Puppy is Not a Current Craze
Research your breed

Deciding to take the plunge and get a puppy is a big decision.
Dogs can live and love for up to 19 years, if you're lucky.
(I groom a 19-year-old Pomeranian!)

It is a decision that should be based on your lifestyle, experience and expectations.

Ask yourself the following questions:
Do I enjoy exercise every day-regardless of the weather? Do I like the challenges and problem solving? Am I keen to understand and facilitate another living creatures needs? Do I have the financial means to support this dog throughout its entire life, come what may? What do I hope to achieve from this partnership?

Now, research your breed research your breeder or rescue and take time to make the right decision. It's a two-way street remember.

Ask an expert for advice before taking the plunge, vets or groomers will be happy to give feedback, and you will be well on your way to getting the perfect companion.

Trained Puppies Don't Bite Children

2

Calm is Better For Puppy
Research your breeder

The first 6 weeks of a puppy's life is usually with the litter and the mother. From the age of 2 weeks their eyes are starting to open, and their ears open soon after. Ideally from this age, they need to be in an area in the house that's safe and peaceful but also exposed to all the sounds and sights of a busy household. Socializing starts at a tender age and correctly done will help tremendously towards having a calm well behaved pup.

A calm relaxed mother will also teach the pups to be calm and relaxed. A nervous mother dog that stresses out or overly reacts to visitors or disturbances in the home will trigger the same reactions in the pups. The fight or flight response will activate, causing undue stress and fear in the puppies. Combined with the genetic component of already having a nervous anxious mother, it's likely the pups are being set up for a lifetime of fearful and stressful reactions, which will be difficult to overcome as the pup gets older. Therefore, ideally you should visit the puppies 2/3 times before you pick one to take home, to make sure all is as it should be. The mother should be calm and relaxed and happy for you to visit with the pups. If there is any growling or the mother needs to be put into another room, I would walk away. The same would go for the father if he is around.

I was lucky enough, with my first puppy Meggie, to visit twice before making a decision. I also knew and groomed the mother and the grandmother, and I knew they were an extremely good natured and healthy line of collies. She is now almost 16, and my wise decision then, has given me 16 wonderful years with a wonderful dog, that my children are benefiting from also.

If you have any concerns that all is not right, walk away. It's better to start with the right raw material rather than trying to correct an already ingrained issue for years to come.

3

Puppies Eat Scraps!
Variety in diet is good

A good base diet is very important for a growing puppy. But equally important is a bit of variety! In fact, trainers who train dogs to do nose work such as drug detection or tracking people, believe that exposing a puppy to lots of different smells and tastes early on, leads to a better sense of smell.

Also, how dull would our lives be if we had a bowl of stew every day for dinner and breakfast for the rest of our lives!

My dogs eat a good, high meat with minimum processing, diet but also get the kids crusts, cereal, and any other safe leftovers.

If you don't want your dog to be a pest at mealtimes leave these treats aside to add to your dog's own dinner or throw them onto a nearby bed or mat. Puppy will quickly learn where to wait and won't keep foraging under the table! I'll admit mine get scraps throughout the day. They calmly lie down close to the table until the tell-tail sound of the fork scraping the end of a bowl.

Remember to adjust the dog's regular food portion to account for an extra treat throughout the day or you will quickly end up with an overweight dog.

If you are feeding a commercial whole food, make sure that a whole type of protein is the first ingredient. For example, chicken, beef, or duck. Also weigh your puppy and be sure you are feeding the correct amount according to the recommended guidelines. And remember to adjust them as the puppy grows. Puppies actually need twice the amount of food that a grown dog of the same weight would require. Variety, in general, is good for a puppy but some common dangerous foods include grapes, raisins, chocolate and onions. Contact your vet as soon as possible if your dog ingests any of these.

Giving your pup a plentiful supply of long-lasting chews and toys stuffed with tasty treats will keep him happy and content. Chewing relieves stress and helps with teething. It also distracts puppy from eating cushions clothes and toes.

4

The Pup Needs Roast Chicken!
How to use higher value food

When starting to get your pup out and about it's important to teach him that YOU are the most interesting thing around, and sometimes roast chicken is the way to go. In the training classes I teach, people will sometimes arrive with dull boring treats, sometimes just the dog's normal food. If your dog is a foodie that's great if that keeps your dog's interest. But most pups, faced with the huge distraction of 5 other puppies and their owners, will need a little extra motivation to keep them focused on their owner.

When I take a young pup out for an off-lead walk, I always take a toy and some high value, smelly food such as chicken. Every time we pass a distraction such as another person or dog, I make myself super exciting and fun and I reward that focus with chicken. The arrival of distractions, rather than being something the pup will run up to investigate, quickly become a precursor to the arrival of chicken.

Over socializing your pup to the extent that they think everyone is going to lavish them with attention is a mistake lots of owners make. A 30 kg muddy excitable boxer is not going to be greeted in quite the same way by strangers as a cute wrinkly 8-week-old pup. It is best to teach puppy what the norm will be when they are young…after all they will be adult dogs for lot longer than they will be puppies.

5

Eat to Feel Fit
Overfeeding pitfalls

Obesity in the dog world in Ireland is at epidemic proportions. Start right with your puppy to prevent a host of health-related issues. A good 60% of the dogs I see in my grooming business are obese and a lot are morbidly obese to the extent their health is being badly affected.

As a new puppy owner it will help to be aware of this and how to avoid it.

Most owners have little idea of what a dog's ideal weight should be or how it feels. You should be able to easily feel, but not see, your dog's ribs and spine when you run your hand down his back. You should not have to search heavily under a pile of fat. It doesn't help that pet food manufacturers will usually overestimate the amounts of food your dog needs. I usually recommend reducing by 20 %, but to continue to assess and weigh your dog and increase if required.

Most vets allow free weighing of your dog in their waiting rooms so avail of this.

Exercise is important too, but I find diet to be the main reason for obesity. It leads to problems such as arthritis, heart issues, skin problems, sores, and a generally unhappy, miserable dog.

Owners will often substitute food for walks or attention. It's an easy trap to fall into with busy lifestyles and one I sometimes fall into after a long day at work. Raw bones, raw vegetables, and treat balls stuffed with normal food portions are healthier ways to give a dog a healthier more satisfying snack. It will also satisfy their natural forgoing and chewing instincts.

If you think your dog may be overweight, weigh him first and compare this to recommended weights for your breed. A quick google search will tell you this. If you have a small dog, you can weigh him at home by holding him and stepping on the weighting scales. You then subtract your own weight. If he is very overweight, you can seek help from a nutritionist, but an easy way to start is decrease the food by 10% and increase the exercise by 10%. Weigh him again after a week and you will know if you're on the right track. If he loses no weight a vet check would be no harm to rule out any medical conditions.

Good luck. Your dog will thank you for it.

6

Don't Leave Your Husbands (or anyone else's) Shirts Lying Around!
Preventing unwanted chewing

Puppies explore the world with their teeth. Anything within their eye view is considered fair game. And why not? We bring them into our world with all our rules and etiquette and expectations, but they are a totally different species. Rather than turn unwanted chewing of items into a battleground, why not simply set the pup up for success by not putting temptation in his way.

For the first few weeks keep all items you don't want your pup to chew up off the ground and away from puppy. Confining puppy by using a crate (zone 1) or puppy pen (zone 2) (more in chapter 9), which has lots of allowable chewing items will teach him what he can chew and prevent him from making wrong choices. As well as the frustration of finding a chewed shoe or belt there is also the dangers associated with puppies getting accustomed to chewing potentially dangerous items, which could get stuck in his airways or digestive system.

As the puppy grows older and has learned what he can chew and gets rewarded for that, he can be allowed into areas that have items around that he can't chew and be interrupted, redirected, and rewarded at (IRR) to reinforce choosing accepted items such as Kong's, raw bones, and raw hides. (More on IRR in chapter 9)

7

Don't Lose Your S*t!
Patience is key

Puppies are hard work, harder than most people anticipate! They are needy, whiney, teethy, chewy, barky bundles of cuteness. A rare combination. Once the initial novelty wears off, after a few days, the hard work really starts.

An 8-week-old puppy will need to be brought out to toilet area every hour and/or after sleeping, eating, playing, excitement or drinking or when circling and sniffing behaviour occurs…phew. And yes, that's a lot of waiting around outside for puppy to 'GO'. And you must wait with him to educate and reward. Unless this hard work is done in the early days and good habits are formed it's going to backfire royally.

Recently I had a customer asking for toileting advice for their 8-month-old Yorkshire terrier boy. They hadn't put in the effort in the early weeks, a common mistake with lots of owners but particularly owners of toy breeds. Owners tend to baby these dogs and allow them to toilet on puppy pads in the house and avoid taking them out in bad weather. Invariably, due to being totally inconsistent puppies never become reliably housetrained. We are saying to puppy, "pee outside puppy…but ok wait if you're stuck or if it looks a bit windy out there it's ok, just pee in the house." Using the puppy pads or newspaper for too long in the home, turns into using mats and soft furnishings, and when adolescence arrives can lead to marking all over the house. This was where these yorkie owners were at.

So yes, be patient, be consistent, and be diligent. Remember we made up these strange rules about where the dog's toilet should be, which may seem strange to a pup, and after all we use a room in the house as a toilet. So be kind and fair in educating him. He wasn't born knowing this and he's not trying to annoy you when he gets it wrong…so don t lose your s*it!

8

Vaccinations Aren't Evil (at least for pups!)
Get veterinary advice and research vaccinating

When born, puppies get immunity from their mother through the milk. This lasts until the puppy is a few weeks of age. At 7/8 weeks, the pup should be vaccinated against the most prevalent diseases. These include deadly parvovirus, a horrific disease that can take a puppy's life in a couple of days. Symptoms include vomiting, lack of appetite, lethargy, and bloody diarrhoea. It is easily transferable between pups through direct contact with faeces. Protection against Distemper and leptospirosis are also included in the standard 7 in 1 vaccination.

Four weeks later your pup should receive a second vaccination. This is important as occasionally the first vaccination can be cancelled out by residual protection from the mother's immunology, via the milk drank as a younger pup.

Most vets then recommend annual vaccinations. Personally, I have mixed views about this. I will vaccinate again a year after the puppies second vaccination, but rarely thereafter. There are many studies that prove that immunity against most common diseases last for most, if not all a dog's lifetime. There is also growing evidence of long-term nasty side effects to over vaccinating. These can happen days or weeks after the jab so it's often hard to prove a link. They occur as the dog's immunity can overreact to the vaccination causing an autoimmune response.

An often-unknown option is to get your dog's immunity level tested prior to vaccinations. This can be done via a titer test which some vets offer. Single vaccinations of, for example against parvo, can be given if needed rather than the full 7 in 1 dose that your dog may not need. An educated decision can then be made whether to give booster vaccination or not.

Speak to your vet and educate before vaccinating.

9

Owner: Don't Stand at the Business End!
Toilet training

Puppies sometimes need privacy when doing the business, i.e., poos. Sniffing and circling are often part of this ritual so off lead freedom is best. Dogs often develop their favourite surfaces, such as gravel, grass, or woodchip. One of my dogs sought small bushes to do his business against.

Vigilance is essential when toilet training your puppy. They should be brought out on the hour, every hour and also: after eating, drinking, waking up, any exciting activity. They should be watched for any signs of wanting to wander off into another room or quiet corner. Try to encourage them to find their own way to the back door-if you carry them, they may never figure out the route!

Verbal praise to a puppy when toilet training is great but from a distance. To keep it simple I have divided the places a puppy hangs out into 3 zones and explained how to deal with toilet training in these areas.

3 Zone Rules

The basics of toilet training means understanding that puppies have in innate desire to be clean. This means that, given the opportunity, they will, from an incredibly young age, move away from their bed/food/resting area, to find a toileting area.

Ideally this toilet area will have a different surface to their bedding, for example grass, gravel, newspaper, ideally something porous. So, we set up their zones based on whether we want them to start to learn to 'hold it' or whether we have to leave them for longer and can provide appropriate access to a toilet area that we choose.

Zone 1

This is a small confinement area, for example a crate or small utility (for a larger puppy). There should be no toileting area available here, just his bed, suitable chews, and toys.

Suitable For:

1. Short term confinement during the day (1 hour maximum), when puppy is tired and has just been played with and gone toilet. This can be increased to 2 hours for puppies over 6 months.

2. Long term confinement at night for the older pup, 4 months and upwards. Most pups this age should be well able to be clean at night for 8/9 hours. Keeping him in the crate at night will continue to encourage it. If you intend to get up throughout the night to let your younger puppy out, he could be placed in here too. When he is not able to move away from his bed to find a toilet he should whine or bark, waking you up to bring him out. This is for hardcore owners. I've never done this, but it will quicken up the toilet training process. Me, I like my sleep too much!

Zone 2

Larger confinement area, for example a small utility or bathroom, puppy pen or outdoor fenced area. It should have access to a suitable toilet area.

This is for longer term confinement, for a puppy less than 6 months, for 2 or 3 hours during the day or 8 to 10 hours at night (if you do not intend to get up through the night)

This area will have a bed, suitable chews, toys, water, and maybe food, covering 75 percent. The other 25 percent of space should have a different surface that pup can use as a toilet area. Inside it may be puppy pads or newspaper. Outside it may be sand, gravel, bark mulch, or grass. Pups, if reared correctly, will naturally seek out separate surfaces to urinate and poo on. Be aware though, if you get your puppy from a puppy farm where it is likely to have been reared in a cramped and dirty environment, these clean habits have not been allowed to develop, making house training much harder.

Zone 3

Puppy is loose in house/garden with diligent supervision and is educated on proper toileting habits. If pup is in zone 3, he must not be allowed access to zone 2's toileting area, if this area is in the house and not where you want the pup to pee/poo long term. So, close the gate or door to this area or remove the newspaper and clean properly.

Dealing with little accidents:

A biologically appropriate cleaner which will effectively remove the smell of ammonia/urine is vital. It's a common mistake to use whatever cleaner is under the sink. This may contain ammonia also and therefore your pup will be attracted back to certain areas in the home to use as a toilet. These will usually be a different surface such as a rug or carpet. These are harder to clean so pup is attracted by his acute sense of smell and will have reoccurring accidents. Take up rugs and mats and use baby gates to limit access to carpeted areas temporarily until good habits are formed.

If you catch pup in the act, Interrupt, Redirect, and Reward (I.R.R.).

This means using your emotions and your body posture and get to your pup as quickly as possible. Your emotions should read shocked and disappointed, your body posture should read alarmed. With a very confident puppy, you can also clap hands and stomp feet!

You should only say whatever word you use to let your pup know whatever they are doing is not wanted or desired. 'Ah Ah' or 'No' are common words to use. But put emotion and disappointment behind it! Dogs learn from our body language and tones of voice; they are not born understanding English. This takes time to teach.

Attaching an emotional response to a word will help them understand the meaning. The word 'Ah AH' or 'No' will serve as a reminder in the future. It will then give your puppy a chance to change his behaviour thus avoiding a negative consequence and giving you an opportunity to educate and reward. Your puppy should jolt and look apologetic but should not be frightened of you or worried about approaching you to 'make up'. If he is, you need to tone down your response to an appropriate level so as not to frighten him. You must then redirect him to where you want him to toilet and reward him for doing so. Education is key, a negative consequence alone is never the solution.

Trained Puppies Don't Bite Children

10

Give Your Puppy a Tour de la Garden
First thing to do with your new puppy

The very first place your new pup should set eyes on arrival at his new home should be the place you hope he will use as his toilet. This will usually be an area in the garden. After the stress of being separated for the first time from its mother and siblings, and usually a car journey with a different species (humans!), they will need to pee and/ or poo. The meeting the family, the selfies, and the cuddles can wait. Start as you mean to go on and set your pup up for success.

I once, unintentionally, left my dogs locked in my home for almost 24 hours. I was on holiday, and my neighbour, who had been minding them, mixed up the time I was arriving back.

I was quite surprised when they bolted for the outdoors when I arrived home late at night. I had assumed they had been let out only 3 hours earlier. We only figured out the mistake the following day. But guess what, the house was spotless. They were so well house trained that even being left for 24 hours hadn't prompted them to break good habits that were so ingrained.

Trained Puppies Don't Bite Children

11

Observe Your Puppy
The importance of learning your puppy's body language

Dogs are a completely different species to us. They are not born understanding our complex society and our social niceties. They of course are born not understanding a word of English but can read body language. If you think about it, body language is the only language common to both species. When immersed in a pet home as a young puppy they should quickly start to understand our emotions and facial expressions too. Commands are usually the last thing they learn through the process of training.

Watching the puppy will give us clues to how he feels and be predictors to behaviours. According to the book which inspired me "French Parents Don't Give In", by Pamela Druckerman (a concise version of "French Children Don't Throw Food", by the same author), American scientists call this "sensitivity" and say it's the most important of qualities in a care giver. For example, stress signals in dogs include yawning, lip licking, tucked in tail, wide white eye, and raised hackles. Just as we expected our pup to learn our rules and traditions, so must we strive to better understand our pup to make his transition to life as a pet dog easier and more enjoyable.

Striving to achieve what the French call "complicate" which means complicity...mutual trust and understanding

12

Tell Yourself the Truth
Understanding breed traits

There is no excuse these days to not research fully the needs and demands of your future dog and be honest with yourself about whether you can meet these demands. No stressful trip to the library is needed anymore to try and find the only book on Chinese Crested dogs. A quick scan on your phone will give you plenty of information. Despite this being the case, I consistently find that the majority of dog owners never do this. For them, how the dog looks is the most important quality they are looking for, and they already know this (probably from pin interest).

I once had a phone call with a distressed owner of 2 English bulldogs, who had started to viciously fight. I asked her to tell me what these dogs were originally bred to do, and the phone went quiet. I gave her a hint: it's in their name…still nothing. I explained how they were bred to bait bulls and to take them down by clamping onto their noses and holding on…not a dog for the faint hearted. And while they of course have not been used for this purpose for centuries, given the correct set of circumstances, these instincts can rear their head again. She was horrified. In her case, they were two unneutered males, aged three and one, and the younger one was starting to assert its dominance. The owner also left them together constantly, allowed them to play roughly together, and spent little one to one time with the younger dog.

All these factors had led to the natural progression to this point - the dogs were behaving in a totally expected and natural way, given the circumstances of their upbringing and environment. Of course, owners simply see this as one problem that needs to be fixed, but unfortunately it is rarely that simple, especially when deep routed genetic needs aren't being met

Learning about what your puppy loves to do naturally, and providing a safe outlet for that, will be a powerful tool to use in your training. When your puppy learns that only you provide that opportunity to catch or chase or tug or search, he will look to you for guidance and give you focus even in the face of distractions,

13

Be Polite to Your Puppy
Meeting your puppy's needs

When you get a new pup, I like to think you are signing a contract with that puppy. As an owner you are expecting the puppy to provide love and companionship, to respect your home, and to follow your rules. The puppy expects you to provide a safe home, good food, and company but also to safely allow him to express his natural instincts. In order to have a calm and respectful relationship it's important to recognize your puppies needs too, which often go far beyond the big 5 - freedom from hunger and thirst, freedom from discomfort, freedom from pain, injury and disease, freedom to express normal and natural behaviour and freedom from fear and distress.

If you want him to lie on the couch and watch Television with you in the evening, you must provide for him physical and emotional needs first. Remember if you want to P.E.T. your dog you must first Play, Exercise and Train.

This can easily be accomplished on one walk with your puppy.

1.On a long line start the walk in a safe location allowing your puppy to explore and feel safe for 5 or 10 minutes.

2.Next take out a toy and play for 5 minutes. If your puppy won't play with a toy, toss some treats for him to chase or sniff out.

3.Walk on the long line for another 10 minutes and then do some training- a sit or some heelwork for 5 minutes.

4.And finish with a 5-10 minute walk on a long line.

14

Don't Overstimulate
Teach your puppy to relax

Puppies need to learn the skill of doing nothing. Like a child must learn the mundane task of waiting in a queue or waiting for his turn to talk in class, puppies need to learn this invaluable skill also. Dealing with frustration will be part of their world, as we must occasionally restrict their freedom on lead. Constantly being amused and entertained is not going to be on the cards. They must have an off switch.

If you want to chill on the couch for a couple of hours and you want to keep the dog in the room, give him something to do to encourage independent relaxation. This could be a safe bone or a stuffed toy. Reward puppy in a calm voice for settling down and not bothering you. You may allow him on the couch or decide he must stay on the ground with a choice of a bed there. Either way, the aim is he is staying out of your personal space and relaxing. For a very pushy dog you could use a crate or tether point to further encourage this through guided learning. This can be phased out over time. Most bad and unwanted behaviour can be built into a dog's behaviour repertoire by allowing the behaviour to go unchecked. Management tools such as leads, crates and baby gates (see chapter 75) can help stop the dog getting this reward and therefore reduce the likelihood of the behaviour being repeated.

15

Nudge Your Puppy Onto a Schedule
Good habits and routines

At first, puppies need to be fed roughly four times a day. Their tummies are still tiny, and they need regularly small meals to keep them satisfied. At around four months this can be reduced to three meals and most owners will settle into one or two meals a day schedule by twelve months.

Some dogs are excellent emotional manipulators and will dictate to their owners how, when, and what they should be fed. If they know the good scraps come after dinner, they are likely to turn their noses up at their plain kibble, causing huge distress to the owner who then takes herself off to the local pet shop to try multiple tasty foods to entice their pooch to eat. These dogs are often labelled picky or poorly. On the contrary they are usually obese and crafty.

Other owners will do free feeding, leaving the food down all day, for fear the dog will die of starvation. I can't imagine how utterly boring this must be for the dog. The same food usually every day, highly processed, and left sitting in a bowl all day. Would you like to be fed boiled potatoes every day and to have to look at a large pile of it on your table every day? Pretty soon you'd never want to see a boiled potato again. Dogs fed in this way often become complacent and uninterested in eating and owners become increasingly frantic about their dog's failure to eat. Owners are also losing out on the valuable tool that food is used to train and motivate your dog. Hard to get a dog motivated about food when he's stuck looking at it 24/7.

Dogs should enhance our life and add quality to it, therefore we shouldn't allow them to dictate feeding times. I've had clients who arrange their social lives and schedules around the fact that their dog demands to be fed at a certain time. My dogs are fed once a day in the evening. This can be anytime between 7pm and 9pm. They fit into my schedule. They get bits and pieces throughout the day, leftovers or rewards for training, so the odd time I have to feed them earlier in the day, I can do this too. This is my schedule. And my dogs adapt.

Figure out what schedule suits you. I would recommend a bit of flexibility around the time but a similar routine leading up to it.

16

Raw Food Isn't Poison
Consider the benefits of raw food

There is a growing awareness that highly processed dog food, usually full of carbohydrates, are not an ideal diet for most dogs. Dogs are mostly carnivores, , but will also eat fruit, vegetables, and 'human' food, given the opportunity. I often have owners tell me how good they are treating their dog by never allowing them 'human' food, when in fact 'human' food is simply human grade meat. And why don't our dogs deserve properly sourced and produced 'human' grade meat? The dry pet food industry begun in the 1930's as a way to use horse meat from horses killed during the war and to profit from by products from the grain industry. Real meat products just weren't available for pet dogs due to rationing. It was never intended to be a permanent solution for dog food. There are many types of processes that food goes through to become the finished product of dog food, and in general the less processing the better. The high temperatures involved in making this long shelf-life food decreases the nutritional levels of the food. If you aren't keen on handling raw food, freeze dried food offers more retention of nutrients. Like human food, the less processing the better.

17

Vegetables Can Be a Pups First Food
Most veggies are ok in moderation

Variety in a dog's diet makes for a happier, healthier, more resilient dog. Owners will sometimes tell me how they gave their dog fresh chicken and he had diarrhoea. They then assume their dog has a sensitive stomach and vow to stick to the bland dry food from now on. When pressed it turns out the dog was on a strict dry food diet up until they tried chicken, with little or no variety. So, it's no big surprise the dog's system was unable to cope. I find having a good quality base food is useful, but I also supplement with fresh meat, fruit, and vegetables, as well as some naughty leftovers. These mean my dogs have developed a robust digestive system and can enjoy vast variety in their diet. This makes training more exciting as I can use jackpot rewards of tasty fresh meat. It also means I have lots of options when giving them stuffed Kong's or long-lasting chews.

 If your dog has health issues or allergies, make sure you seek advice from your vet before making any changes to his diet.

Trained Puppies Don't Bite Children

18

Understanding The Science of Being Alone
Teaching the skill of being alone

When your puppy is born it usually has the company of its littermates immediately. For the first 5/6 weeks it will probably never be left alone. But in ideal conditions he will be learning a bit about being left during this time. In a properly set up puppy pen the mother dog should easily be able to leave her pups without them being able to follow. She will need to use the toilet, and as pups get older and grow teeth, she will spend less time with them as she readjusts back to her life, enjoying time with her owner and getting walks.

From three weeks when their eyes open, puppy will see mommy leaving, but this mild stress will be counterbalanced by having each other for company. A good breeder will also handle each pup and do gradual periods of separation for each puppy. So by eight weeks when most puppies leave for their new homes they have some experience of being left alone and although the move to a new home will still be a bit stressful, they have some experience and confidence of 'standing on their own two feet' and that even if they are left alone, someone will always come back.

These puppies adapt much quicker to being left, although it is still wise to do this gradually and carefully over a period of a week or so.

Being ok with being left is a learned skill. In the wild a dog may never spend time alone. They are a target for other predators and are viewed as potentially being injured or vulnerable in some way.

We bring our pet dog into a world where we need them to deal with many frustrations and confinements in their life, such as kennels, confinement, and isolation at overnight vet's visits and grooming appointments. So even if you have another dog or plan never to have to leave your dog, teaching this skill when the puppy is young means less stress down the road (for you both!) if the circumstance arises. Having a dog which cannot be left alone could also lead to an abundance of problems such as separation anxiety, barking, destruction, and stress.

19

Puppies Can Be Noisy During The Day Too
Learning the skill of 'in-room' separation

I regularly get calls from clients who have puppies, who while fine during the night sleeping alone when the house is quiet and everyone else is asleep, refuse to settle behind a barrier during the day. Covid may have a lot to do with this as many owners have been working from home, with new puppies having full access to them during the day. As they get bigger and more boisterous, this becomes more problematic.

From a young age it is very useful to teach your puppy to handle separations from you, via a crate or a baby gate. Make sure they are tired and content and leave a novel, new, long-lasting chew or stuffed toys for them to enjoy. Graduate from being in the same room to leaving for short periods and returning. Keep leavings and returns low key and don't acknowledge your puppy. It should be no big deal and he should barely notice you have left. Visits to vets, groomers, and kennels will be much more bearable for your puppy when he learns to be calm and relaxed when people leave, as they will always come back.

Trained Puppies Don't Bite Children

20

Practice 'La Paws'
How to deal with attention
seeking behavior

This was one of the most useful tips I picked up from reading the aforementioned book. It referred to the 'pause' you should do before racing in to check on why your baby is crying. It gave your baby a chance to self-soothe and put himself back to sleep without a crutch. It is similar with puppies. It is especially important that puppy learns early on that cries for attention are not rewarded. This is not the same as ignoring your puppy.

Teaching your puppy to be content spending time alone is a skill they must learn and must be taught with compassion and empathy. Older puppies may try to experiment with boundaries and try some attention seeking barking when left.. For example, you pop him in to a crate or behind a baby gate for thirty minutes while you have a shower (or try to!). If you go back the second, he makes a noise, even in some cases to reprimand him, he has been rewarded simply by your presence. You must try and wait at least two minutes. This is called a disassociation time. It means when you return after two minutes of quiet, puppy learns it's the quiet calm behaviour that causes your return, not the crazy hysterics!

If left unchecked as a puppy, destructive behaviour when left can continue into adulthood, often resulting in a dog being surrendered to a pound. Rushing in to check on your puppy will only reward that behaviour and potentially result in attention seeking barking.

Puppy barks, owner returns, result: puppy barks louder and for longer until owner returns. Even if owner is angry, the dog still gets attention and company so in a lot of cases, they will take the hit in order to not be alone.

Make sure puppy isn't being triggered by noises or movements outside a window or other dogs. Having his bed in a quiet secure area helps puppy feel more secure and safe. Leaving plenty of things to chew will relieve stress and give puppy something to do to help him settle back to sleep. If you are sleeping with your puppy during the first few days so as to bring him outside to toilet, you must of course bring puppy out when he wakes. But keep it low key and calm to encourage him to go back to sleep soon after.

So, remember the two minutes 'le paws'!

21

Set The Mood For Sleep and Time Alone
The Importance of Routine

Routine is very important for puppies. They, like babies, thrive on knowing what's going to happen and when. It is especially important as we cannot communicate this through speech, as we eventually will with our babies. So, they rely on it so much more.

My evening routine, while not set to an exact time, is as follows. (It's not important what the routine is, once it's nothing that will hype puppy up too much, it's the ritual of it as a prediction to sleep that is important).

They will have been fed around 8pm, after which they are let out into garden. I usually read a story to my girls, and then after a bit of housework I have an hour of Television. The dogs will be allowed to join me on the couch, and we all relax together. At around ten I let them out again, and they can hear me feeding the cats and getting myself ready for bed. I get a treat ready for them, a stuffed Kong maybe or a pig's ear. I try to have something which will last. Giving them something to chew in their beds relaxes them and releases dopamine to aid sleep. I drop each dog's treat into their bed, and I let them in. I say, 'night night', with little fuss, and take myself off to bed.

I find having a set routine but not a set time also works well for the morning. School mornings, we are up at 8am, but it can be nearer to 10am on a good weekend. My dogs never bark to be let out in the morning. They are familiar with the routine, and they know that barking for attention will never be a predictor for my arrival (Or at least never a pleasant arrival!).

Similarly, my dogs know by the shoes and jacket I wear if I am leaving them at home for a short while. They will (usually!) already have had a walk and be tired, and I toss a long-lasting chew or Kong into their beds, and they don't even make any attempt to follow me out the door. With a different jacket and shoes on they would be beating down the front door, barking and circling in excitement!

My dogs settle best at the back of the house where there are no windows to look out over a busy area.

When puppies don't learn this valuable life skill it can end in disaster. Owners with multiple dogs will often not think to teach a new pup this skill. They may have a very tolerant existing dog that allows the new pup to cuddle up to them at night. The pup has effectively found a replacement for mum, and/or his littermates. Owners may only realize they have a problem if the older dog's dies, or the puppy needs to spend time in a vet or a kennels.

As a groomer I have had to witness very distressed and frustrated dogs try to cope with simply being in a crate alone, while being able to see other dogs around. They have never been taught to be alone or to deal with stress, and therefore any level of confinement is hugely stressful and frustrating for them. I have had dogs injure themselves and even get their jaws caught on the crates, and in that case the owner hadn't even left the room! We had to get someone to cut the wire to get him free. Thankfully he was unhurt. In this dog's case, he was an only dog, and had learned to spend time alone, but it was always on his terms. He could freely roam the house and watched everything outside from his thrown at the top of the couch in the living room. This dog did not strictly have separation anxiety, but he was allowed to get away with blue murder and was lord and manor of the house. Dealing with frustration was not part of his life. Barking usually took care of any obstacles. He did learn to be quiet and settle in the parlour with me pretty easily. But as soon as the owner arrived he was back to his old tricks.

Trained Puppies Don't Bite Children

22

Try The Training Cure
"Stay" - the training steps

Teaching your puppy a basic stay can help with control at doorways when off lead and safety when getting out of a car. It also helps provide them with a cue when you are leaving them. If your dog hasn't the self-control to stay when you ask at a doorway it's going to be much harder to leave him. He'll be worked up and stressed before you pull out the driveway.

To teach a good stay, tether your dog to a solid object (radiator is handy). Put their bed there too if you like, and make sure they are tired. Now put six treats in a line in front of him, but just out of reach (I know, the cruelty). Stand about two feet in front of the treats, upright with no food on you (very important part!). Now simply wait. Most dogs will try their hardest to reach the treat. Most will use their paws or wine or bark. Just ignore all behaviour, keeping a neutral expression on your face and wait. Eventually your dog will stop for a couple of seconds and not move. Immediately smile, praise, and pick up a treat and give it to him and return to your spot. At this stage it doesn't matter what position he is in. Even if he's standing on his head, if he keeps position for two seconds you need to reward.

Your dog should quickly work out what he needs to do in order to get you to cooperate. Build up the time and give calm, gentle praise when he is getting it right. After a few repetitions you can introduce your word of command, usually STAY, and a hand signal can help also. Eventually you can stop tethering but it still helps to leave the reward for the dog on a counter or shelf, so he is less interested in wanting to follow you.

Using a stay command when you leave your dog can signal what's about to happen and help your dog understand that you are leaving him, but it's no big deal…and you'll always come back.

23

Coping Alone Is Better For Puppy

Get puppy used to spending some time in a kennel environment

Dogs should enhance and enrich our lives and fit in with our habits and schedules... Once fully vaccinated, getting our puppy used to spending overnights at a trusted kennels or minders will make life a whole lot easier on both the owners and the dog's life. I have met owners who haven't had a holiday in years, or even a weekend away for fear of upsetting their dog.

Well-adjusted puppies adapt pretty quickly to changes in environment and form friendships with new caregivers pretty easily. So, while we would like to think he won't cope and will cry in the corner for the whole time, a good kennel will usually bring them out of their shell, and with new walks to enjoy and maybe other friendly dogs to greet, most dogs do just fine in kennels for brief periods.

Everyone likes a break away from the mundane responsibilities of life every once in a while, and much as I adore my own dogs, I admit to also enjoying the odd dog free holiday. It makes you a better, happier person and a better dog owner.

24

Trust that your puppy will grow up!
The cons of resorting to punishment

The first six months of a puppy's life are difficult. A positive outlook, empathy, and understanding is very important and will go a long way. The opposite type of person is unfortunately out there too. I recently hung up on a prospective client, my first time ever hanging up on someone (at least in my professional life!). She had an 8-week-old puppy she had gotten from the local pound. (The only positive in a conversation that went downhill almost immediately!). She was having difficulty with housetraining, and after shouting at the puppy wasn't working, had decided to go out and buy an electric shock collar. This was a tiny Jack Russell puppy. Now the puppy was doubly frightened of going to the toilet when new owner was around. He got shouted at, and now a sharp pain was mysteriously being felt on his neck every time he tried to go to the toilet. The owner had now successfully taught the puppy not to dare go toilet in front of her.

By using punishments first, she had lost the opportunity to teach the puppy where the toilet actually was, i.e., outside on the grass. She rang me, when after a half hour walk with the pup, when he didn't go toilet, he promptly let go and peed the second he was back in the boot of the car, and the owner was out of view. The owner was utterly convinced that the puppy had a vendetta and was doing it on purpose.

Needless to say, we had words and I hung up. Thankfully a few weeks later I heard she had given him up and he landed safely at a good rescue. Who knows what kind of damage that pup would suffer long term, not only in terms of house-training skills but on the damaging and fearful relationship with people he was forced to endure as a vulnerable puppy.

So be kind, be fair, be your puppy's best friend and role model, and you should come out of the puppy days in one piece.

25

If you miss the window for prevention, you must treat Dealing with parasites

Unfortunately having a puppy also means having to manage and treat a variety of parasites. These includes worms, ticks, fleas, lice and mites.

Young puppies are particularly vulnerable to worms, which can cause severe intestinal issues and fleas and ticks which can cause anaemia.

A mother dog can easily pass on these parasites to her puppies A regular worming schedule for young puppies is very important, so speak to your vet for recommended treatments.

Many spot-on flea treatments work very well at repelling fleas and ticks easily, however do some research on the potential side effects as with any medication.

More natural deterrents such as garlic and diatomaceous earth can work well also.

A healthy dog with a good diet will naturally have better immunity against parasites.

26

There is Time for Guests
How to teach your puppy to accept guests in the home

All dogs need to learn that visitors to the house are not a threat. This is especially important with breeds that have been bred to have stronger guarding traits. For example, German shepherds Pyrenean Mountain dogs and Dobermans. However, without guidance, most dogs will show some natural inclination to warn of a stranger's approach. When my puppy is young and visitors come to the home, I like to have him safely confined into the utility room with a high value long lasting treat. I want him to be able to hear and smell the visitors without feeling like he is at risk. After a few minutes I will open the door to allow him to see me with the guest but keeping him safely confined in a crate or behind a baby gate. Puppies are good at reading our body language and if they see us from a safe distance hugging, embracing, and smiling at the visitors this will give him a good clue as to whether this visitor is friendly or not. After a few minutes if the guest is happy to meet the puppy I will bring the puppy out, usually on a lead and with a toy or an exciting chewy to divert attention. I want to create a happy balance between the puppy greeting the visitor and being happy to see them but also remaining calm and not pestering them. I want the puppy to learn when visitors come it is a good thing as it signals that their favourite toy or favourite stuffed Kong will come out also. Bringing a young puppy to the front door in your arms or on a lead can be very overwhelming and scary so it's better to wait to do this when the puppy is older and when the guest is familiar.

27

There's Just One Bone A Day
The cons of free feeding

French children generally stick to set mealtimes and don't graze constantly throughout the day. The opposite of this for dogs is free feeding. This is when a dog's food bowl is left constantly filled up for him to help himself to throughout the day, and often the night too. This can cause many problems throughout a dog's life. When they are puppies it means it is harder to predict bowel movements as you never know when he has last eaten. If puppy gets sick it will be difficult to assess when and if he has last eaten. It also makes training sometimes difficult as food is now so freely available that its stock has plummeted. Why work for something when you get it for free just by being pretty.. I often think, as it takes the ritual of being fed out of the dog's routine, that you are taking away an exciting time for the dog and a chance to bond and train. There is also the behavioural aspect to consider. For your dog to respect you and form a close bond you must control and supply all the things he needs to survive. If you simply hand over all the food, you are tipping the balance of power over to rovers' side. A pushy, more dominant dog will see this as a weakness on your part and may try to control other resources in his life , such as toys, people or sleeping areas

28

Don't Solve A Problem With A Treat.
When food becomes a bribe-recall pitfalls

As a more 'positive' dog training movement takes over the dog training world, the option to say 'no' to your dog seems to have been obliterated. Don't get me wrong, I view myself as 95% positive in my training methods, but that leaves a good 5% for good old common sense.

If my dog is misbehaving, for example, has ignored my command to come, (even though this has been trained very well and he should know it), I'm not going to run over to him and try and entice him with a treat. This is using the treat as a bribe and not as a reward. You run the risk of the dog learning 'when I ignore commands I get food', which is of course the polar opposite of what you want. Firstly, I would use my voice to issue a new command, in a more serious tone, such as 'leave it'. If he still finds the smell more interesting than me, I will use I.R.R. (Interrupt, Redirect and Reward see chapter 9) I will then take a few steps away and call him to me, now giving him a chance to make the right decision. His body language should read 'apologetic', but he should not be frightened of me. I will reward with praise, (voice and touch), but I will save higher value rewards, such as treats or play, when he responds first time. My dog has learned, when I ignore my owner, she gets lighting speed and becomes extremely disappointed. When I come immediately, she is incredibly happy, and we have fun. If I had just used a treat to lure him back, he has learned to follow a treat and that if he ignores the recall command, good things happen.

29

You Are The Keeper Of The Property
The importance of having a secure area for your puppy

A secure garden is essential when having a dog in your life. Unfortunately, the old Irish way of life allowed for the casual wanderings of the neighbourhood mutt. And there are plenty of owners, both city and country dwellers that still allow it. It is my biggest pet peeve and it brings me back to my very first dog training house call.

It was to a rural home that had taken in a stray collie pup, about six months old. Looking back, I realise they were never fully committed to keeping the dog. If it worked out (with minimum effort from them), great, but if not, it was no big deal (at least not to them).

It started poorly. The dog was not even on the property when I arrived. Too late I realised this was what I called a 'free roaming' dog. Left to their own devices to roam wherever they pleased. They were usually difficult to train as they were self-reliant. They were usually fed in a few different houses, and made their fun with other loose dogs, or worse, things to chase like cars, bikes, joggers, or livestock.

The problem with this young collie was that he was nipping the kids' shoes as they ran around the garden. Obviously, the collie was doing exactly as his genetic make-up drove him to do, and in the absence of any authority figure to tell him otherwise, or give him an acceptable output for this behaviour, he figured the kids were the most fun.

I started teaching him to target his chasing instincts on a thrown toy, which he learned amazingly fast. If we were going to stop the children chasing, we needed to provide him with an alternative outlet, one we could control. Otherwise, he would likely start chasing cars or sheep. I used a long training line to discourage him from chasing the kids and taught them to be boring and still. He learned very quickly that nipping the kids was not an option and was happily chasing and retrieving the ball.

The following day I heard they had dropped the dog into the local pound. The father, not having been at the training session, let him out of the garage that morning without the training line on and he promptly went back to what he enjoyed - nipping the kid's ankles.

I rang and tried to rescue him, but as the owners had reported him as having bitten a kid, the poor pup was killed.

So, the moral of the story, keep your dog safe and on your property. It is, after all the law (Control of Dogs Law, 1986) but also, it means you can control access to the things the dog needs and loves, such as food, water, companionship, play, and instinctive behaviour, thereby strengthening your relationship and control.

30

Make Your Dog Your Best Friend
Why you shouldn't 'baby' your puppy

Hundreds of thousands of years have been devoted to making Canis familiaris our best friend. Dogs have adapted and learned to want to please us, protect us, and be our lifelong companion.

In recent years there seems to be a trend to reverse this. We seem hell bent on demoting them to baby humans. How could we be so egotistical to think another species (especially one as loyal and amazing as the dog), would WANT to be treated as the baby of an entirely different species. But still we now hear owners referred to as 'guardians' or 'pup parents'.

Dog kennels are now called doggie hotels, with overnights referred to as doggie sleepovers. We wouldn't dare leave our pup at home for longer than a couple of hours. No, it must be dispatched to doggy day care to meet all his doggy friends and get socialised. Apparently eight weeks with his doggy siblings and mother has taught him nothing. How on earth do wild dogs survive without this extra vital socialisation? There is doggie hair dye, doggie nail polish, doggie prams, doggie clothes, the list goes on.

If we want to have a wonderful relationship with our dog (and sadly a lot of dog owners don't really see this as a priority), we need to be their best friend and companion, not thirty other dogs we've never met. We need to be their best friend, role model, playmate, and disciplinarian all rolled into one, not unlike my relationship with my children.

31

Serve Consequences Swiftly
How to inhibit puppy biting

Puppies nibbling your fingers is totally normal behaviour for them but of course is something we wish to discourage. When a puppy is biting my fingers, I will firstly give him a warning 'ah ah', whilst simultaneously acting like he has really hurt me (even if he hasn't) using a low disappointed tone. He should back away and look a bit surprised, but not frightened. I then produce something that is fun to chew, such as a toy or a rawhide and reward him lavishly with smiling, praise, and petting for making a better choice. I will always have this better option available to him when I am hanging out and playing with him. I will aim to keep my hands still and boring and the toy exciting and unpredictable.

If your puppy is particularly bolshy and goes back to chewing fingers, I would now go straight to eviction. Again, say 'Ah Ah' (more loudly this time), and place puppy outside, or in a room on his own (which of course is puppy proofed). Being deprived of your company and evicted from the family should make him rethink his actions prior to this negative consequence. It is important to give him the 'ah ah' warning first, as this will remind your pup of the consequence of ignoring this, i.e., the eviction.

32

Everyone Does The Same Thing
Don't be a sheep-be your puppy's voice

People find it very hard to resist the lure of a cute puppy. When you bring your new puppy out in public, random strangers will often bear down on you staring intently at your puppy while making cooing noises and petting them on their heads. If people did this to babies, they would be arrested or at least have some very stern words from the mother. Puppies can find learning about this strange new world and the people in it a bit scary. When they are restricted and restrained in your arms or on a lead, they don't have the space or the choice to move away in order to feel safe. Of course, you want your puppy to learn that people aren't scary but, you want to find the balance so that your puppy is comfortable with any encounters. Generally speaking, with my puppies, I would arrange meetings with friends and family in a safe setting where the puppy can be off-lead or at least on a long line to greet or move away as they see fit. In public with strangers, I would just allow the puppy to observe, and I would reward all calm, relaxed observations with food coming from me. It can be hard to speak up on your puppy's behalf in public, but I find a cheery 'no thank you, we're training' and an about turn with a tasty treat on your dog's nose can be a better solution for all.

33

You Just Have To Train It
"Recall" - the training steps

Many owners have difficulty with the recall command. This is a command that should communicate to the dog immediately, 'stop what you are doing now and come back here fast'. It is one of the most important commands you can teach your dog, helping to effectively control the dog both inside and outside your property.

Many owners mistakenly think that because they have given their puppy a name, that he should know when you call his name he should come. Unfortunately, this is rarely the case, mainly because you may say the puppies name several times during the day. 'Honey, did you feed Molly?', 'Where is Molly?', 'Molly, I'll murder you', etc. It does not necessarily communicate to the dog what you want them to do which is, 'come here now'.

So, while you can use the dog's name to get her attention, you must follow it up with an actual word of command. This might be COME or HERE, or even a whistle. And you must take the time to link this word with a behaviour. And the behaviour must be the puppy running to you in anticipation of something fun happening, usually food, attention, or games.

There are 3 steps to training a recall.
1   The command – come.
2   The behaviour - dog running to you.
3   The reward - treats or toys.

The reward should be high value food, given while simultaneously praising lavishly.

The behaviour can be encouraged by having a helper restrain the dog on lead, showing him the treat and moving a few paces away and enticing him to you with your body language. If working alone you can toss a treat to create distance then produce another one to encourage the recall behaviour. Additionally, anytime the puppy is running to you happily expecting good things to happen, you can add the command as the behaviour is occurring.

Confusingly though you start at stage 2 - getting the behaviour. If you start to use the command too early, without the dog carrying out the behaviour, it will dilute its meaning and effectiveness. Every time the dog hears the word COME, it must be doing that behaviour. That's how the dog's brain forms the link between the word and the action. And of course, what drives that behaviour to be repeated is the quality of the reward, step 3.

34

Keep Jackpots In The Mix
The beauty of random rewards

Did you know, gambling is similar to dog training?

Well, it's hardly surprising that you wouldn't let me explain how they are by telling you my 'whole roast chicken story', which I tell in my training classes.

Imagine the scene. Your dog is eighteen months old and is generally well behaved and obedient. You are finishing a long walk at the beach, and walking back toward the pier, when suddenly a van opens and eight labradoodles run frolicking and playing down to the surf, right in front of your off-leash dog. He takes in the sight with wide, excitable eyes, and not believing his luck, takes off at speed to join in the chaos. You don't react for several seconds, so unexpected is the scene, but you jolt yourself back to reality and holler. 'Oscar, come here.' The sight in front of you is one to behold. Oscar has almost reached the surf party, when upon hearing your command, skids to a halt, sand and surf thrown in a halo around him. He spins around, back feet rooted to the spot and races at top speed back to your side.

So, what should your response be?

Put him back on the lead and put him in the car?

Give out to him for running off in the first place?

Or tell him he's a good boy and give him a pat on the head?

Neither of these responses is correct but the third one is nearest to the correct answer. The reward here should justify the amazing recall your dog just did. Faced with the prospect of a sea and surf party with a pack of manic labradoodles, he chose you. You need to acknowledge and react to that, so he keeps choosing you.

So, you must immediately, without delay, produce from behind your back a whole roast chicken (bones removed!) and present it to your dog. Do you think now he's likely to want to repeat his amazing recall? Most definitely, because you have now introduced the element of surprise of jackpotting to your training. He will strive to do better and work harder in order to receive that wonderful jackpot again.

Now unfortunately, we are sometimes ill prepared for that wonderful response we get from our dog. It may not be recall, but maybe he sat calmly by your side while you enjoyed a coffee in town, or he did a full walk without pulling on the lead or resisted jumping up on the visiting kids. You can jackpot with your emotional response, physical response, an extra exciting game, or multiple treats. Be inventive and exciting and your dog will become addicted to training, like how a gambler gets addicted to the high of the jackpot win in the casino.

35

You Choose The Walk; Your Dog Chooses What To Sniff.
The importance of sniffing for your puppy

A dog's sense of smell is 100's of times stronger than ours. It teaches them about the world, all the things in it, as well as important information about other dogs he may encounter.

Male unneutered dogs will usually take more of an interest in smells. Often even licking the area to try and decode its meaning. Is it the smell of a young enticing female? Or a bigger, older male? Its behaviour will be driven by what he discovers from the behaviour of the other dog. It may simply be air scent your dog detects or sweat glands from the other dogs' paws. The easiest way that dogs leave information for each other is of course through urine, and dogs will be naturally driven to leave their own mark near the scent they have discovered.

I am always saddened when owners complain to me that they have stopped walking their dogs as they are fed up with him stopping to sniff, especially if it's an unneutered male. The dog is doing what nature dictates he does, both to survive and to procreate. Neutering should help to lessen this, and females, unless in heat, are usually less interested in sniffing. Your breed of dog can also dictate how much sniffing they like to do. Dogs which have been specifically bred to track will of course naturally track on a walk too and become obsessed by smells. This includes basset hounds and beagles. I believe a compromise should be made with sniffy dogs. Part of the walk they must 'leave it' and keep walking, but you make part of the walk 'free time' where they can sniff, either off lead or on a long line, and just enjoy the experience of being a dog and letting them be led by their nose. Your dog will be more content and fulfilled after this experience, and therefore be more likely to settle and relax at home when you return, so it's a win-win.

36

Socialisation, Variety
The Differences between
Socialisation and Habituation

Socialisation

Puppies, go through a critical period where they need to learn
that other species, including humans, are not to be feared and are
in fact part of their family. They learn to react socially with other
living creatures. This applies to any animal you want the puppy to
potentially live with, for example, rabbits, horses, pigs, any animal
that you want the puppy to accept happily as part of normal life. This
period starts as early three weeks and closes around sixteen weeks.
Any species that the pup hasn't been correctly exposed to before this
time period, is likely to invoke suspicion and alarm from the puppy.
If the puppy is older and confident when this happens and the other
species, for example a chicken, gets spooked, its likely to end in
disaster.

The play drive of a puppy can very quickly develop into a prey drive
and end up with a mauled or even dead chicken. This is especially
true of dogs which are specifically bred to hunt prey, such as
sighthounds.

Habituation

Habituation is the process by which a pup is exposed to all the sights and sounds and things he is likely to be exposed to for its lifetime. This list is endless including different locations, different sounds, different terrains, different environments, and different modes of transport. This starts as soon as the puppy's eyes are open and will continue for the dog's lifetime, however the influential first few months are the most critical.

The overall aim for habituation is to gradually expose your puppy to these things in a calm, relaxed manner, so they are no big deal. The clue is the French word, s'habituer which roughly means, 'getting used to things'. For example, being aware of the sheep in the field and the trains on the tracks but it's no big deal to the dog. It's neither exciting nor frightening. They are aware of its presence, but they don't care.

It's not always easy to get this 100% correct and even with my latest dog we hit a roadblock. She had been going to dog shows from a very young age and was confident there, until suddenly, for no apparent reason, she would become very anxious, not engaging in play, and either trying to climb on my lap, or trying to pull back to the car. I was baffled, and I admit, frustrated the first few times it happened. After all I had gotten up at 6 in the morning and trained for months and now, I had a dog I couldn't even get in the ring. It took me a few weeks to figure out the trigger. The trigger was people clapping at the presentation of awards. Now these were small presentations with only a handful of people around, but obviously this was not something I had prepared her for.

37

Dogs Drink Water
A basic requirement

Well, this is obviously true for all dogs. Clean fresh water should be available all the time for your dog. It is the law. Clean the water bowl regularly otherwise it will become stagnant and develop a slimy look. There are no excuses for failing at this vital commitment to your dog. He is utterly dependant on you for his survival. If you notice your puppy drinking a lot more or less than usual, do seek medical advice.

38

'Looks' Matter

Encouraging engagement in public

From an early age you need to encourage your pup to pay attention to you, especially when on walks together. I am always disheartened when I see puppies dragging their owners around on lead, getting agitated and excited when they see other dogs or running children, anything exciting really. Your job as a puppy owner is to teach your puppy that these things are no big deal. It's not enough to physically prevent him from being rewarded by these things, you must convince him that you are much more fun. Encourage focus on you with energetic games with toys or food. Make him want to look to you for all the fun and engagement on a walk. Otherwise, you will soon have a full-grown dog who may get too strong to control around distractions or one who may resort to frustration behaviours such as barking, lunging, or biting the lead.

39

Talk About Anything
Socialising pitfalls

When out and about socialising your puppy, try not to focus on cramming in as much as you can. Of course, you want to try and expose puppy to as much as you can, but if you go overboard, you may overwhelm your puppy. Keep it calm and relaxing and gently talk to and encourage your puppy along. A word of warning though, there is a thin line between gentle encouragement when a puppy is feeling a little overwhelmed, and inadvertently rewarding behaviour which may be linked to fear. Watch his body language carefully and aim to 'jolly' him along and reward him for being brave, rather than scooping him up and consoling him. (However, tempting this may be!)

40

Keep The Days Habituation Balance In Mind

Educate for the puppies lifetime, not yours

While you need to keep the process of habituation light and breezy for the pup, it's no harm to keep a record of what your pup has experienced and has not. You can find useful lists of socialisation and habituation scenarios online. Be particularly aware if you live in a quiet area to still try and habituate the pup to busy traffic, and vice versa if you live in a town. Remember all the 4-legged animals in fields that your pup needs to see and ignore. This may require more effort in winter months as livestock may be indoors. I have had to socialise my puppies in wintertime and would randomly stop the car wherever I saw livestock and let my puppies watch them from a safe distance, often from the car. I walked my dogs on county roads usually surrounded by cattle, but they were sparse during winter. Remember to socialise for your dog's life, not your own. For whatever reason he may not end up with you for life and may have to cope with many different environments. So, if you live in the countryside, make an effort to bring your puppy for trips into town for short walks in a more built-up environment.

41

Socialisation Shouldn't Involve Mouth To Mouth Combat
The cons of overenthusiastic puppy play

Unfortunately, there is a huge misconception among puppy owners that their puppy needs to meet and play with many other puppies in order to be correctly socialised. If you mentally change the word 'socialise' to 'learn to mostly ignore', you will get a more accurate idea of how socialising your puppy to other puppies should go. In fact, by the time your puppy gets to you, he should already have almost finished his socialisation around other puppies. He should have spent about eight weeks with his litter mates. It is really the process of habituation around other dogs that he needs to master. He needs to 'be aware but not to care'. It is far more beneficial for your pup to meet friendly adult dogs that he can learn to greet appropriately. If you have a very bouncy confident puppy, it really helps if they meet a few well socialised adult dogs who will very quickly but kindly show him his place. No one wants their puppy to grow into a thug. If this confident puppy attends lots of 'puppy parties' or play sessions with lots of other puppies, he will very quickly become a bully.

Any games which involve teeth on skin should especially be avoided. It's called play 'fighting' for a reason and can quickly escalate as such. If you must allow your pup time with other puppies, try and encourage play around toys (this will keep their mouths occupied). A good general rule (and somewhat deterrent), would be for every half hour your puppy plays with other puppies, he must play with you for an hour and a half (not all at once obviously!). His bond with you must override all other relationships.

42

Be Free
Give your puppy some choices

It can be easy to get caught up in all the pressures of trying to get socialisation, habituation, and training all in a short period of time. Remember though your pup needs time to switch off on a walk and just be a dog too. I divide my walks in training sessions, play sessions (these often overlap), and time 'off' just to be a dog. Once they stay relatively near me, they are free to sniff, explore, pee, run, jump, and just enjoy being a dog. They must still return to me immediately if I request it, and not bother any other dogs or people, but they are essentially off duty. This freedom of choice makes the walk stress free for the dog (and the owner!).

Trained Puppies Don't Bite Children

43

Keep Meals (out) Short And Sweet
Eating in public with your puppy

A good exercise for puppies is to learn to be calm and well behaved when you are having a meal. Set your puppy up for success by having him tired, well exercised, and recently fed. Not many places in Ireland allow dogs inside but most allow dogs to accompany their owners to outdoor eating areas. For your first outing, choose a quiet area and bring your dog's blanket and a tasty stuffed Kong of bone. It helps to practice a bit at home too first. Puppies can learn a 'settle' command or a 'down stay' to help them learn to relax in these scenarios. If puppy is overexcited and risks jumping up on your (or others) table, you can stand on his lead, or tether him so he is comfortable standing or sitting, but the lead will prevent the upward motion of a lunge towards the table. Using a chain lead will prevent chewing. Keep it short and discourage anyone from approaching him while he is resting.

44

Don't Train Your Dog How To Dance

Leadwalking issues with a puppy

You will be training and communicating with your new pup for every day for the rest of his life (hopefully!), so take the time to teach the most important stuff first. These are usually toilet training, play with a toy, and recall. This is setting your pup up to have an extremely solid relationship with you. This in turn will give him more freedom and fun in life.

I get many clients complaining that their puppy won't go on walks with them and refuses to move. Of course, he does. He's a tiny puppy and you're trying to drag him away from all the safety and anchor of his new home. Don't rush him. I tell these clients they will be ringing me in six months complaining that the puppy is now pulling.

I find it easier to put puppy in the car and park up somewhere to walk him, armed with his favourite toy and some treats and preferably a safe offlead romp on a long line You then become his anchor and security blanket and he will be keen to follow you. Alternatively carry your pup outward from the house and walk him back to the comfort and security of the home.

Safe off-lead (but on a long line) walks are much better for puppy and allow time for play, training and engagement which go far beyond just holding a dog lead and walking.

45

Let Your Dog Set The Pace
Some breeds are 'smarter' than others

Different breeds develop at different paces, and let's face it, some are blessed with more looks than brain cells (yes red setter I'm talking about you!). There is a reason you won't see a setter making it as an assistance dog or a drugs dog. They do make wonderful therapy dogs though.

Every dog and every breed of dog has different strengths and weaknesses. Some are bred to be more independent thinkers such as liverstock guarding breeds and terriers. Some will pick things up immediately and others will need more repetition and time. And of course, the type of reward you use will depend on what that dog enjoys doing. (More in chapter 47). Try to keep sessions less than 15 minutes long and end when puppy is still keen. Keep them fun and exciting.

46

Teach The 5 Magic G.I.R.L.S.
My top 5 training exercises

Every trainer has different rules and boundaries that they set for their dogs. The important thing is not really the actual rules but how consistent the trainer is in enforcing them. Like children, dogs flourish by knowing their place, and therefore feeling loved and protected. When I started to put my list together for this book I found, ironically that they made up the acronym G.I.R.L.S. I have twin daughters and currently own 5 female dogs.

Here are my 5 top training expectations I have for my dogs, to help ensure the relationship is fulfilling for us both and mutually beneficial.

G is for Git. (Chapter 79) This basically means 'sod off I'm not available to you right now'. I would use it if I'm resting on the couch and they are pestering me for a cuddle, or if I'm holding a toy or food on a walk and they are off lead, bouncing around in front of me anticipating a game. It is especially useful for the girls to use too so the dogs learn to respect their personal space. It also eliminates problems such as jumping up and nipping clothes.

I is for In/Out. (Chapter 80) This means I can easily command the dogs in or out of a room or a crate or outside on a walk. It is basic good manners.

R is of course Recall. (Chapter 33) This means in any scenario at home or out in public I can call them back once and they will immediately return to me.

L is for Leave it. (Chapter 87) This means that I can tell them to move away from something I do not want them to approach or have. Again, it applies at home and on walks. Examples include dropped food items, dog poo, other dogs.

S is for STAY. (Chapter 22) This means I can get my dogs for stop moving (any position) until I give them a release command. This might mean moving them off a path to allow bikes to pass on a walk or at home to teach calm behaviour at the door.

47

Let Dogs 'awaken' And 'discover'

Why breed traits decide on rewards

In the child version this means allowing children to learn about 'sensory pleasures' (it's not as naughty as you think!). It means allowing them time to explore the world around them and learn to 'discover' their bodies. In my class I ask the owners to research what the dog (or in the case of a mixture, their dogs) was originally bred to do. This will give us lots of clues to what rewards we should utilise to reward him. For example, for a border collie it may be the chance to chase a ball. A basset hound would value the opportunity to follow a scent, and for a Labrador, of course, the opportunity to swim is usually a valuable reward. By using rewards that we know will fulfil both a genetic predisposition and be 'sensory pleasurable' for the dog, we will foster a stronger bond with him and allow him the sheer joy of experiencing the things in life he was selectively bred, over generations, to excel at.

Using toys to play with and reward our dogs is far and beyond the best way to develop a strong bond. All the top handlers in the police, agility, obedience, know by using the reward of toys, they will get the best results and focus from their dogs- which is what the pet owner wants also.

Trained Puppies Don't Bite Children

48

Leave Time For Trust
How to be your dog's security blanket

Some dog owners (and parents!) are so permissive with their dogs, that the dog ends up very insecure and neurotic. Owners cannot understand this, believing as they have indulged the dog's every need and adore him so much that he must therefore feel loved and protected. The opposite is more often the case. By indulging a dog to the point that he can do and act anyway he sees fits, you lose all respect and authority.

How then can you expect your dog to trust you to protect him, both in his home and outside of it?

The result is most of these dogs are stressed out and on edge nearly all of the time. They are alert to every sound and sight outside and inside the house. They pull their owner around on the lead, and are alert to everything on a walk also. They rarely listen to their owner and are forced to try and make decisions and influence their environment in scenarios for which they are usually set up to fail. For example, the postman comes every day, the dog chases him off, but he keeps coming back day after day to 'torment' the dog. The dog is left home for an hour and rips the bottom of the door off in a bid to be free to protect his house. When you readdress this relationship and how the dog views you, it's the equivalent of putting a nice cosy security blanket around your dog. You are taking the burden of decision making off your dog's shoulders. He can't cope with it anyway and it's stressing him out.

I've seen dogs go almost immediately into a deep sleep when an owner starts to take back control, the relief for the dog is so immense. There are very few pet dogs out there that are naturally dominant and confident enough to take on the role of protector and decisions maker in the home. And it would be very frightening to live with one.

49

(Don't) Let Puppies Socialise With Puppies Their Own Size.
Pitfalls of too much doggy play

If you take the easier (lazier) route such as play with other dogs (requires no input from owner, except to end the fun and drag the pup away), you will inevitably end up with a dog that has little interest in you and seeks out other dogs at the earliest opportunity on a walk. Remember, dogs playing is commonly referred to as 'play fighting', why do you think that is?

Dogs that practice rough mouthing during 'play' with other dogs, will, if (and when!), they end up in a fight, react and fight in the exact same way. They have been rehearsing this behaviour during 'play' sessions. These dogs inevitable end up in a fight as they will generally be allowed to run up to any dog they meet to 'say hello'. Other dogs, especially on lead dogs will often not appreciate this invasion and will react accordingly. After a few minor tellings-off the dog now still runs up to other dogs but is now on edge and defensive, which is a recipe for disaster. The sad thing is most of these dogs inevitably end up being given to a rescue or a pound, or restricted to on lead walks only, or worse, no walks at all.

I'm not saying dogs should never be allowed to play together, it depends on the dogs, and the style of play, and in my mind the dog must only be doing it because he doesn't have access to play with you. You must come first as the dog's play mate and role model.

50

Back Off (And Quieten Down) At The Training Session
Don't repeat commands

Sometimes when training you need to back off and let your puppy figure it out for himself. By repeating commands, you are only teaching him that he doesn't have to listen to the first command, and by trying to manoeuvre him into a certain position, he will usually push back against that pressure and then become confused about what you were actually trying to tell him.

I recall reaching a dead end with my dog Tilly when I was teaching her the clear jump for I.K.C. Working Trials competition. It involved getting her to clear a 3 ft jump on command. I was getting too involved in the training, trying to 'help' her, and getting frustrated when she wasn't getting it. Being a sensitive collie, she was picking up on this and was starting to go under the jump. I needed to take myself out of the equation and let her figure out what I required from her. So, I put the jump out, about 1 ft high and I sat in a chair beside it with some treats and said nothing. By a system of trial and error, she eventually figured out that when she popped over the jump, I tossed her a treat. After a few sessions, her confidence was back, and she was happily clearing the 3 ft.

Less is sometimes best with dog training.

51

Extracurricular Activities Are For Pleasure, Not Competitive Advantage
Focus on your dog, not everyone else's

I compete, at different times, in working trials and obedience and agility competitions.

A friend of mine once commented that I needed to pay more attention to my competitors and what they were doing with their dogs, with a view to figuring out how to beat them. I told her I didn't care what my competitors were doing, and that as I saw it, once the dog and I performed to the best of our ability then that was all I could ask for. A rosette was of course a bonus. And that's not to say I don't want to win or place in a competition...I absolutely do. I often make notes of things that went wrong at a show and practice to make sure they don t happen again.

So, while its healthy to take an interest in other people and their dogs, constantly comparing your dog with someone else's is unhealthy. You get out what you put in, and every dog will develop at a different pace.

52

It's Not Just About Results
Enjoy the special moments

At the end of the day, my dogs are first and foremost pets and companions. It can be easy to lose sight of that, especially if you have hit a roadblock with a training issue. Our dogs will not be here forever and in most cases, we will outlive them. I treasure my lazy Sunday morning where the kids have radiated towards the tv room and the dogs and I can enjoy a leisurely breakfast in bed. They get to enjoy a few crusts at the end, and lots of cuddles too. I honestly think they would sometimes be happy to stay like that forever.

The French call these precious times 'moments privileges', little pockets of joy or calm when you can simply appreciate being together. With a common-sense approach to training and leadership you could enjoy many years of these with your dog.

53

Give Your Pup Lots Of Practice Of Waiting
Learning self-control

We live in a world where (most) of us have to queue in a line, or wait on hold on a call, or (back in the day), wait patiently for the internet dial-up to finish. We have to learn to deal with this or we would live a very frustrating stressed-out existence. The same is true for dogs. We need them to accept being on a lead, wearing a collar, being confined on our property, spend time in a crate, being handled, and restrained.

These are expectations we place on our dogs, without really thinking about how alien it must be to the dog. Left to their own devices they would never have to experience these restraints and frustrations. So, it is important to teach your puppy to happily accept these inevitable events from an early age.

A simple exercise when they are young and on a collar and lead, is to throw a treat or toy just out of their reach. Say nothing and ignore the barking, lunging, and attempts to get the treasured item. Just wait. And when puppy relaxes the tension in the lead and gives up immediately tell him okay and drop the lead, encouraging him to get the item. Over several repetitions puppy will learn that calm patient waiting behaviour gets better results than crazy puppy hissy fits. This will filter out into other scenarios too to help puppy cope better with the life we need him to not just tolerate but enjoy.

54

Slow Down Your Response Times
When overindulgence backfires

This one won't go down well with some puppy 'parents' out there. The French call it an 'obligatory passage, in which the child learns she is not the centre of the universe'. It can be an easy trap for owners to fall into, especially if they have no children themselves or are empty nesters. It can be easy to treat puppy like a spoilt child that needs to be constantly indulged and pandered to. You have to think that some owners enjoy this sense that their dogs would be so stressed and miserable without their constant attentions and indulgences. And some dogs can quiet happily fill this role of king or queen of the household without exploiting the situation or become stressed out with the pressure. But many more do become extremely stressed and anxious with the arrangements, with anything new or different being like a huge mountain to overcome.

Dogs thrive on leadership and direction to help them feel safe and secure. Indulging and pandering to their every whim can be a slippery slope to go down. When I meet a very stressed out dog and I explain why the dog is stressed out they often feel defensive and confused. They think that because they adore the dog and let him do whatever he likes in the home that the dog should be happy. They often come to me regarding issues on a walk, such as reactivity to other dogs or people or recall issues. They don't connect how their failure to communicate and control their dog in the home is of course affecting their control of the dog in public. Most of these dogs feel unsafe and are insecure and trust no one to keep them safe. Walks outside are terrifying. These dogs are crying out, not just for love, but for someone to take control of an environment they find scary and have little control over.

55

Expect Dogs To Appreciate Body Language
Smile, praise and pet when delivering a treat

When we use food to reward a dog during training it can be easy for the dog to quickly value the food over the owner. When you start to fade the reliance on food or move to other types of rewards you might find your dog's attention and enthusiasm start to wane. Therefore, I like to teach 'smile praise and pet' as you are delivering the food treat. This forces the owner to show their pleasure at the dog's behaviour in ways other than food. And it teaches the dog the link between the primary rewards, food, and the secondary rewards, our owner showing they are pleased with their body language, voice and emotions.

Therefore, when we start to vary the reward and the reliance on the food the dog should have learned the joy of making us happy with their good behaviour and not just the joy of a treat.

56

Don't Let Your Dog Interrupt
Good habits need
to be formed from the start

Good manners in dogs are as important as good manners in children. Some people are so wrapped up in the 'needs' of their pups, that they forget that they will have to live with the bad habits they have allowed to develop. And these habits, which may be seen as cute or funny in a small puppy quickly lose their sparkle when you are faced with a fully grown dog. For example, a tiny puppy growling at the postman, barking for attention, or being jealous of a partner can be viewed as funny or cute, but laughing and indulging this behaviour will only reinforce it and it will continue to occur. Even after the novelty wears off, the behaviour has become ingrained and any attention at all (even negative) might be deemed a successful outcome for the grown dog.

Teaching patience and manners starts on day one when puppy comes home. Don't be under the misconception that he will 'grow out' of certain unwanted behaviours when he magically turns a year old. You'll be sorely disappointed, and a visit to your local pound will prove this. Remember the old saying, 'what you learn first, you learn best'.

Trained Puppies Don't Bite Children

57

It's Mutual,
Don't Interrupt Your Dog
Let sleeping dogs lie

This is true in certain scenarios. For me that would be when the dog is sleeping and eating. The old saying 'let sleeping dogs lie', can sometimes be forgotten, in people's expectations for dogs to put up with whatever they decide they should. During lockdown in 2020, I had several calls from owners, worried about their dog's strange behaviour. There were comments on dogs growling when approached when resting, usually coupled with reports of the dog 'acting strange' and taking himself off to sleep in unusual places. One even took sanctuary in a cupboard. These dogs were being subjected to the 'love' of their owners all day long, instead of just three or four hours. They wanted some peace and quiet.

By all means if you have to, call your dog to you if you need him but avoid disturbing him by encroaching his space. He could be in a deep dream and react out of fear and misunderstanding. I believe it is the same at mealtimes. Owners sometimes actually create food guarding issues by taking their dog's food away, mid meal, to 'show him who's boss'. This is archaic training advice that will only serve to make your dog uncomfortable with you approaching his food. Get professional advice if your dog is growling in his bed or around any food, as the wrong approach will only make the matter worse.

58

Observe The Food Rules
Extending good behaviour

Delaying gratification is a lesson in dealing with frustration. As I mentioned before, it is a valuable life skill in dogs and children, which has to be taught. From a dog training perspective, this would involve moving from a fixed system of reward, for example, every time the dog sits, he gets a treat, to a variable system of rewards, he only gets a treat for the quickest or the longest. This teaches the dog to offer better and longer behaviours in order to get the reward. The best rewards should be kept for the best behaviours to keep him motivated and keen. These are called jackpot rewards and might include extra tasty morsels, multiple treats given in a fun way, an exciting game with a toy, or all the above! Behaviours such as a SIT/ STAY, and any behaviours need to be proofed with distractions and different locations. Constant praise and encouragement for getting it right can always be given via calm, gentle praise and by smiling at your dog. This feedback is invaluable and helps to fill the void of the expectation of the food treat.

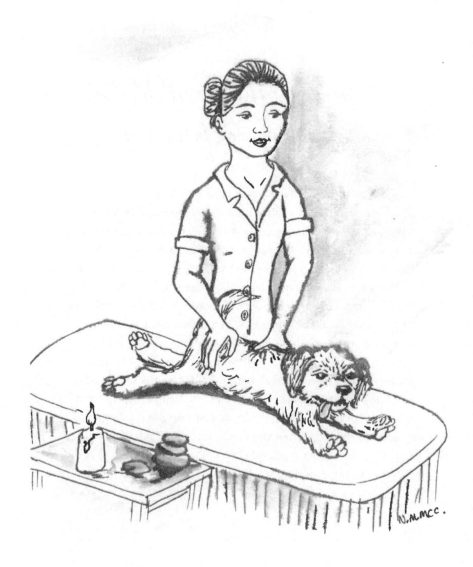

59

Let Them Eat Scraps
Patience is a muscle

If there are any scraps left from our dinner, that are safe for dogs (and most are!), I will put them aside in the dog's bowl, to mix in with their normal food portion later that day. The dogs know this is happening, and one in particular, Meggie, will happily lie in the kitchen, facing the microwave, where the food is, for hours. She doesn't guard it or demand it, she will just quietly settle down, safe in the knowledge that the time will come when she gets to enjoy it. This is another example in a lesson on patience. She is 16 years old and has been practising this behaviour for years. Patience is like a muscle; it needs practice and eventual reward in order to master it. Years of positive experiences have taught her that calm, relaxed, behaviour will be rewarded.

Trained Puppies Don't Bite Children

60

Treat Coping With Eviction As A Crucial Life Skill

How removing your dog from the room can decrease unwanted behaviour

Dogs learn best when the consequence of an action occurs immediately after the event. For example, when you want to teach your dog to sit you will place a food treat on his nose and the very second his bum hits the ground, you will release the treat. Because you are adding something positive to a behaviour this will increase the likelihood of this behaviour reoccurring. If the dog is doing something you do not want to occur again you can add something the dog perceives to be negative to try and decrease that behaviour. There should never be a need to physically harm or terrorize your dog when doing this. The simple expression of emotion coupled with the exclusion from the family should be enough for most dogs. Eviction should never be the first training tool you use especially with a young puppy. Positive reinforcement training and management tools are an important aspect of training, but real-life scenarios are likely to occur where immediate action is needed for the dog's safety and for the safety of others living in the home. A short house line is a useful tool to have on your dog if you think you're going to need to use eviction. An example would be a dog who persists in stealing food from countertops. When you catch him in the act of stealing, clap your hands, stamp your feet as you approach the dog and give a loud sound of disapproval. Pick up the long line and unceremoniously escort your dog out of the room. You should leave him to 'marinate' for at least two minutes in a place which is of course safe, but where he feels a little bit lonely. When you allow him to rejoin the family be aloof and calm and as always make sure to verbally reward any better choices that he makes.

61

Cope Calmly With Tantrums
Grooming and handling skills

Every dog, regardless of coat type, needs to learn to calmly accept grooming and handling. They may need regular professional grooming or clipping, or ear/eye drops, or a cut cleaned, or a splinter removed. If you wait until you have something potentially unpleasant to try and restrain and handle your dog, he will likely rebel, and even if he cooperates, he has now learned that handling equals something potentially unpleasant and may be less inclined to cooperate in the future. I recommend teaching them to accept and even enjoy handling from a young age. I set them up for success by tethering my young dog to a solid object and gently pulling them towards me by the hips so that the lead his taunt but not tight. This will prevent him from turning around and nipping. Gently handle him all over, just with your hands, checking ears, teeth, feet, and tail. If he stands quietly, give him calm, gentle praise throughout, and after 2 minutes, untie him and immediately reward him with his favourite thing, an extra tasty treat, or a game or a walk. He will quickly learn the association between these handling sessions and a great reward. If, in a more likely scenario, your pup struggles and objects, it is important not to give in to this tantrum. I have known dogs to even go into 'death rolls', in their bid to dislodge you. The trick is to hang on. If you release your pup as soon as he resists, you are rewarding that objection. Once your pup has no behavioural or medical conditions, there is no reason why they can't simply stand still for a couple of minutes while someone they should already trust, handles them gently. Make sure when the tantrum is over that you get two minutes of calm behaviour before you release them and reward. Once they are already good at coping with frustration and delayed gratification, you can also put the reward in front of them, just out of reach to help them focus. Remember tantrums don't change the rules and as the authority figure in the house, you should be able to inspect your dogs. In short, be calm and sympathetic, without giving in.

62

Being A Role Model Requires Leadership
Multi-dog household issues

Most of us would like to think that we, the dog owners, are top of the hierarchy structure, and it's important that our children come next, followed finally by the dog. But in multi-dog homes, it's important that we recognise and support the social structure there too.

Meggie, my older collie, is a kind, placid dog, wonderful with kids and people and very biddable and respectful. In the dog structure, she is an excellent boss. She is unwaveringly confident in her position which means she has never had to fight to keep it. When her daughter Tilly was born, I worried as I knew mother/daughter conflict in the dog world could be devastating. Thankfully Tilly lacked the social ambitions of her mother and was happy to play second fiddle. Meggie, once she realised, when Tilly was about 6 months, that her daughter would be hanging around a lot longer than she would have liked (she did the bare minimum as a parent!), She 'dive bombed' her several times. This involved playfully running at her and barking, forcing Tilly to give passive, respectful body language. It never happened before, and never happened since. They pretty much ignore each other to be honest. But it was written in stone from that day forth that Meggie would reign as queen of the dog family.

When I got Cassie, who was a half-sister of Tilly (same father) and the most confident of a litter of 7, I did worry a little. I knew the first year would be ok. I knew my dogs wouldn't appreciate a new pup, but (unlike a lot of dog owners who get a second dog), I had gotten this puppy for me, not for them, so regardless of their feelings on the matter, she was staying. I was worried about what would happen when Cassie reached maturity. There was almost twelve years between her and Meggie, and she wasn't a walkover like Tilly. When she was about a year and a half, there were a couple of tiffs, and had I not handled them as I did, they could easily have escalated. They were over food, a nearly empty food container I had given to Cassie. On reflection I have should have anticipated Meggie's reaction and put Cassie in the safety of the crate to enjoy her spoils. But at any rate Meggie arrived in, and being the queen that she is, simply went over and took it off her, delaying the inevitable outcome by growling or posturing was beneath her. Cassie, having grown in stature and confidence decided to object and a minor scuffle ensued. I ran from the next room and assessed what had happened. Of course, my first instinct was to take the prize off Meggie and give it back to Cassie. That was after all, the 'fairest' thing to do. Cassie had it first. But I remembered in time to put emotion aside and side with Meggie. To keep her in power I had to be seen to support her, otherwise Cassie may think she had the support to take her on and become top dog, and I didn't believe that would be a good outcome. So, I scolded Cassie verbally and hunted her out the back and left Meggie to enjoy her prize. There were a couple of these scenarios, but because I handled them correctly and supported the top dog always, Cassie is now four and there haven't been any issues between them since.

63

Give Dogs Meaningful Jobs
A busy dog is a happy dog

Many people will comment on how well behaved and calm dogs such as guide dogs, assistance dogs, or therapy dogs are. Yes, in most cases they will have been brought up correctly with a good temperament and good training, but the dogs are also doing a job and using their brains. Dogs want to be useful and productive; we have selectively bred many of them to fulfil a need in our lives. We expect collies to herd sheep, we want German shepherds to guard our premises, and we want spaniels to flush and retrieve game. In a pet home they have little opportunity to fulfil these needs. Giving them a job that mimics what they would naturally want to do or rewards them with that, will enhance their lives and make for a calmer, happier dog.

Examples may be getting your springer spaniel to retrieve your mail, allowing your setter some free time chasing birds on the beach, or rewarding your jack russell with a squeaky toy mouse. Or better still allow him to catch some real vermin. My dogs must carry their toys in their mouth on our walks, after we have finished playing with them. They will drop them to smell something interesting and I sometimes have to send them back to collect one they have forgotten, but this job keeps them out of trouble on a walk and gives them a focus and purpose which they enjoy. On a walk recently I met a man with a

Jack Russell terrier off lead. The terrier was carrying a large stick and he passed by my dogs showing no interest and engaging. This was a perfect scenario for me as I do not allow my dogs to greet strange dogs on a walk in any case. Later on, we passed the same man and the terrier but this time the terrier had no stick in his mouth. Upon seeing us he immediately started barking and charging towards us. The owner was nowhere insight and after making his point he ran off to rejoin the owner. This owner was totally oblivious to the drastic change in the dog's behaviour when he simply had a job to do on the walk.

A dog that constantly mouths the lead can be cured by giving them something to hold on a walk, a toy or a plastic bottle or even a second lead. It is usually gun dogs who like to do this, and they are so proud to be providing this valuable service on their walk.

Remember the analogy, PET. Before you get to relax with your dog on the couch after a long day's work, you must Play, Exercise, and Train him, so he is tired and content, just as you are after a hard day's work. It's only fair after all.

64

Build Your Dog A 'cadre'
Rules- with a little leeway

In loose terms this means giving your dog a framework of how he should behave. According to Druckerman, the French believe in having a few strict rules but having a little leeway within them. This is a parenting style that I think I had already adopted with my dogs and what really drew me to the book. The French strive to be very strict about a few key rules but also to give them as much freedom as they can handle In dog terms I have my five main rules or expectations, my G.I.R.L.S., but within this, I allow them a good deal of freedom. They are not allowed to sleep in the bedrooms, but can sleep on the couch. They cannot bark for attention or disturb others sleep in the night but they can bark at the doorbell and people going past the house. They can't steal food from surfaces but they do get titbits (just for being pretty) throughout the day. They are not allowed jump on strangers but I allow them to jump up on me. Others may be horrified at allowing their dog to do these things, but for me, once they do all the other things I ask and listen to me, I want them to have some freewill to enjoy our home and enjoy making some decisions themselves. Every household will have different rules and expectations for their dog. Every household is different and that is ok. The important thing is, whatever they are, to be consistent and never to give in.

65

Every Dog Needs To Dig A Hole
Let your dog let off steam occasionally

The French recognise that children sometimes need to let off steam and swear. The child version of swearing is 'caca boudin', and within certain limits , they are allowed to use it. They recognise that kids, like dogs, are subject to lots of rules and frustrations and sometimes need to let off a little steam. For a dog this may mean taking themselves off to dig a hole, doing crazy running circles around the house or garden, barking at birds in the garden, or trying to swim in their water bowl. They are little activities that the dog will choose to do on his own to maybe let off steam or vent some frustration. One of my dogs loves water and at the first sign of a puddle in the garden she will be off sticking her nose in it and digging. She is part poodle so I know there is a genetic component driving this behaviour and it is highly rewarding and enjoyable for her. So I put up with a little mud in the house afterwards, safe in the knowledge I have let her enjoy being her. Within reason, and once these behaviours don't become obsessive or bother anyone, let your dog choose to de-stress in these ways, and appreciate he'll be calmer and happier afterwards.

66

Your Dog Cannot Benefit From Time Away From You
Doggie day care

Using day care facilities for a young puppy can, in some cases, encourage your puppy to view other puppies and dogs as the most fun thing in the world. This can sometimes escalate into frustrative reactive behaviour when encountering dogs on lead on walks with the owner. They don't understand why there is suddenly a barrier to this fun activity, which they have free access to in day care. They can also end up getting a fright around other dogs and becoming fearful. Ask yourself would a dog walker be a better option to break up a puppy's day, if you have to work a long day? Your puppy is getting one to one attention from a friendly human, enhancing his circle of human friends and learning more about our body language and emotions.

If you do allow your puppy some time playing with other puppies try to encourage mouths on toys using extra-large tuggy toys and remember to not allow this activity to replace your games with your puppy. The minute he chooses a game with another dog over a game with you, you are heading for trouble.

67

Be The Referee
Adding a puppy to a household with an older dog

If you have an existing dog in the home and plan to bring in a new puppy, be prepared for a less than warm reaction. Many 'only' dogs are very happy with the status quo and do not appreciate an annoying puppy intruding on its quiet life. Some dogs are of course more tolerant (and even thrilled) than others but prepare to be the referee and protect your older dog from the attentions of the puppy. Most puppies will of course gravitate towards the dog, they are the same species after all, but you must carefully supervise all encounters and don't leave them unattended, at least at the start. This is as much for the benefit of the puppy, as the older dog, as their priority at eight weeks is to learn all the strange different and new body language, language, and customs of humans. Imagine you had to start over living in a country where you didn't speak or understand any of the language or customs. Now imagine if after 3 days of stress and confusion, you met someone who spoke your language and understood your customs. Wouldn't you cling to that person like you would the sides of a rollercoaster? This is how a puppy might feel when they come to a strange house and spot another dog.

Unfortunately, some people get a second dog, as they have found themselves less committed to spending time and walking the existing dog. The second dog is brought to try and fill that void. The second dog invariably ends up with dog-to-dog issues and with owners having little control or influence over him.

68

Keep The Relationship In Perspective
Train - don't assume puppies 'know'

When people get a young puppy, I often get calls about how they can stop their dogs behaving a certain way. They tell me the puppy knows he shouldn't do this, but he does it, and the puppy is behaving badly. These people are expecting a dog who speaks a totally different language to understand the rules in their home.

There are different levels on which you can educate your puppy on proper behaviour in the home.

For example when you want your puppy to understand to be calm around visitors you may encounter three different scenarios

Scenario one- When you are prepared and you have the time and willing helpers. You may bring your puppy into a room on a lead and you may encourage the guests to ask your puppy for some calm behaviour such as a sit or a down and be rewarded by the guest.

Scenario two- When you are not prepared and you do not have time and your guests aren't dog friendly. In this scenario you are much better off ensuring your dog does not learn bad behaviour such as jumping up and barking and pop them into another room with some kind of long lasting chewy or enrichment.

Scenario 3- If you have guests calling who are not dog friendly but you want your dog to learn to be calm in their presence. Keep your dog on a lead and reward calm behaviour or use a tether point or crate in the room and give your puppy a long-lasting chew or stuffed toy, instructing the guests to ignore the puppy.

69

Raise A Praise Addict
Desensitising and counter conditioning

When a puppy or dog gets a fright it may be necessary to try and desensitize them to whatever frightened them. When my dog Riley was a puppy she got a fright when a large Springer Spaniel raced towards her in the park. The spaniel was only chasing a ball that unfortunately had been thrown in her direction, but she thought he was aggressively pursuing her and bolted in fear. Afterwards she became quite fearful of strange dogs, especially when on a lead and would bark in alarm. As I intended to use her as an agility and obedience dog, it was essential that she was calm and felt safe around strange dogs. It was my now my job to try and replace that fearful experience with many many good and neutral experiences around strange dogs. I went to an area of my local park where dogs are mostly kept on lead. I sat on a bench and armed myself with a squeezy tube of dog pate. I allowed her to watch the dogs going by at a distance in which she felt safe and wasn't barking. Desensitizing is often paired with a process called counter-conditioning, so I now paired her experience of 'seeing a strange dog' and not reacting with the positive link of some dog pate. My aim was to change how she feels about strange dogs into something positive rather than something negative thus reducing her need to alarm bark. This process takes time and patience but she is now at a place where barring the sudden appearance of a strange dog is relaxed and calm in their presence.

70

Encourage Puppies to Create Distance Well

Learning about critical distance to fearful things

When dogs are on a lead and they feel threatened they will often bark. This bark is usually high pitched and may be accompanied by lunging behaviour. Owners will often misinterpret this reaction as true aggression. However in the majority of cases this is a fear based reaction and is essentially the dog calling out 'give me space I want to get away from you'.

If you were trying to work on this behaviour using counter conditioning and desensitizing you will need to figure out at what distance your dog can be exposed to the fearful person or thing and not react. This could be anything from 1 meter to 30 meters. It is important to figure this out as this is the distance you will need to start your process. As the dogs confidence improves you can decrease the distance to the trigger.

It is useful to also note that many fear-based reactions are intensified when the lead is tight and when the dog is in front of the owner.

Working on loose lead walking and positioning yourself in front of the dog during a potential fearful event can drastically reduce the chances of your dog reacting.

71

Watch For The Click
The arrival of hormones

In parenting terms this is viewed as a time when something 'clicks' in their mind. When dogs reach a certain age, this happens in lots of ways, but the most important could be the time they realise they have reached maturity and may try and assert autonomy. Dogs with a history of rough play fighting with other dogs, may, upon maturity, realise there are other motivations now for this close physical contact with other dogs, mainly sex. Mounting behaviour can become more prevalent, with both males and females, and other males. Unneutered males may be viewed now as threat and competition rather than playmates. However, any behaviour that a dog has practiced regularly and enjoyed, will be repeated. The brain connector in the dog's mind will make this inevitable. So, the dog will likely initiate the 'play' behaviour, only for it, with the onset of hormones, to quickly result in a fight. And if you took a snapshot of the fight and a snapshot of the dogs previously 'playing', it would look almost exactly the same. It's a tricky age requiring a repetition of training important commands such as recall, stay and leave it.

Trained Puppies Don't Bite Children

72

Don't allow your dog to become complacent
Train at home first

Many behaviour issues that owners experience stem from a lack of foundation training in the home. For example, a dog that lunges towards other dogs on a walk will often be allowed bark and lunge at passers-by from a window indoors or a boundary gate. A dog that jumps up on strangers on a walk may be allowed to jump up on people in the home. Or a dog that gets frustrated or excited by movement on a walk may be allowed to chase birds in the garden all day long.

Remember that any activity your dog enjoys he will most likely try and recreate, even in other locations.

Training begins at home, where there are few distractions and where you can set yourself and your dog up for success.

I fell into this trap with my two youngest dogs. They had spent more time than I would usually have allowed in a front garden where they could see over a road. I was having work done on the house and the quieter back garden was unsecure. On a couple of occasions when off lead, they had charged, barking at other dogs. Now they never played with or greeted strange dogs and were naturally a bit shy so for a while I couldn't figure out why this behaviour had emerged. It was only when I witnessed them confidently 'chasing' dogs which were passing on the road, from the safety of the garden, did I realise my mistake!

Start with the G.I.R.L.S. at home and build engagement and focus which will then carry through to more control when in public.

73

Respect Your Dog And He Will Respect You
Your duty as a dog owner

Dogs in general can control very little in their lives, especially in public. They must wear leads and obey commands and house rules. And yet, in most cases, they continue to be devoted to their owners. They forgive missed walks, long isolations, untreated medical issues, neglected coats, and banishment to a garden, to still yearn to trust and look up to people. Images of severely neglected dogs wagging their tails in the arms of their rescuers will attest to this. They ask for so little and yet give utter devotion and loyalty to anyone lucky enough to be seen as their owner. Remember owning dogs is a privilege, not a right, and we have a duty to care for all aspects of their physical and emotional health for the privilege of calling them 'ours'.

.

74

Guilt Is A Trap
Don't throw in the towel

Evidence now shows that the average age for a puppy to be given into a shelter or pound is eight months. So, owners, after only having this puppy for about 5/6 months, decide that that puppy no longer deserves to be part of their family. There are, on occasion, some very good reasons to rehome a dog, but in my ten years of experience in rescue, including 9 years running a rescue, the reasons were rarely, in my view, justifiable. They included the dog not tolerating rough play from kids, wondering off the property, barking in the garden, not being house trained, nipping the kids in play. All, in my view, human issues, not dog issues. Things that with a little training and advice, could have been easily fixed. However, that would still have been missing one vital ingredient – effort. That is something a lot of pet owners are unwilling to commit to.

In the Druckerman book this chapter refers to the guilt parents may feel at having some child free time and how wasteful that time is if tinged with guilt. I wish more people felt guilt at dumping their dog at a pound or rescue, but in my experience they rarely do. I never remember once getting a call to ask how a surrendered dog was getting on. And in the pound some owners even left with a new puppy after callously dumping their older 'problem' dog that they had no time to try and fix. Teenage years are tricky in dogs, just as they are in children, but would you go ringing social services at the first sign of trouble? Of course not! So please do not do it to the dog. Like teenagers, it is a phase that with the correct approach and training, the dog will come out of, and you will be left with many years of solid companionship and loyalty.

75

Show Your Dog That They Can Have A Life Apart From You
Long lines and house lines

Management tools are important during the tricky teenage months of your dog's life (already much easier than the actual human teenage years right). In smaller breeds it can start at 6 months of age, it is usually later in bigger breeds. A dog is usually considered mature and fully rounded at around two years age, a bit younger for the smaller breeds. So, for example, the teenage years in a jack Russell may be from 6 -12 months. Or in a Newfoundland, between 12-18 months. It is not an exact science, but it is a time when puppies become sexually aware, more interested in other dogs and the smells they leave, and more confident and independent. Some breeds will try and assert their autonomy more than others. I have to say I barely noticed it in my collie girls. My boxer cross, Oscar, was a whole different ball game. Going back to using a long line for training means you will maintain control over your dog, even if he ignores your recall command to approach another dog. A long line is a 6 –12 meter lead used to allow the dog freedom to enjoy "off lead" time, while working towards teaching a reliable recall. It can be picked up at any stage to remind the dog you have control and to prevent him from running up to other people or dogs. Fights can easily break out during this period and it is essential your dog is not put in this position, as it could result in dog-to-dog issues for the rest of his life.

In the home a short house line can be used similarly. If your newly confident puppy refuses to get off the sofa when asked (with a command you have already fairly and kindly taught him), do not turn it into a potential conflict you may not win, simply pick up the line and haul him off. You win and you haven't risked him growling or showing his teeth and you losing that encounter by having to back away. It's important you maintain your role as leader, but you should never have to resort to pain or fear, especially when a simple lead and collar combination will get you what you want.

Trained Puppies Don't Bite Children

76

Birthday Parties Are (not) For Dogs
Do not spoil your adolescent dog

If you continue to treat your 'fur baby' like a spoilt child into his adolescence you will undoubtedly run into problems. Like the stroppy teenager, your young dog will start testing boundaries and seeking independence. It is your job, as his owner and mentor, to continue to remind him that you make the rules, and for his own safety and wellbeing, he must abide by them. The consequence of not doing this, usually means, at the very least your recall will suffer. Many dogs see an end to their off-lead freedom (and sometimes their lives), as they reach adolescence. Owners are unwilling or unable to adjust to this new headstrong dog, no longer cute, biddable, and cuddly. Many dogs don't live to see their first birthday and many others spend it in a second or third home or in a pound. So do your dog a favour and step up to be the role model and authority figure he needs, so he does get to celebrate his first birthday with you.

Trained Puppies Don't Bite Children

77

Lose The Baby Option
De-sexing your dog

Most pet owners will decide to neuter their pet, and in most cases I agree that this is the best course of action. However, your dog must be fully developed before this is done as the hormone changes after neutering can affect how bones develop and can cause pain and lameness later on. Ask your vet for advice.

There can be some drawbacks to neutering. If you neuter a male too soon they can smell differently to other dogs and encourage unwanted attention. Neutering a male dog who is very nervous can make him even more nervous as you have removed the testosterone, a hormone which increases confidence, from their body. Neutering a bitch increases the testosterone so can make her more confident. You should research before neutering strictly for behavioural reasons.

With dog-to-dog household conflict, if you neuter all the females for example, you are likely increasing all their status by the same amount. Neutering only the most dominant female will help the situation better, as it will make her more confident and assertive and less likely to be challenged. The opposite is true for a similar scenario for male dogs-the most confident dog should be left intact and the less confident castrated. This will increase the distance in their status and decrease conflict. Neutering will most likely not affect most behaviour issues with people. It will simply stop a male dog wanting to find and mate a bitch. It can help because other dogs won't perceive them to be a threat or nuisance and therefore this will help lessen aggressive outbursts from other dogs. This in turn will make him less stressed and more content.

It Is important to understand that your dog's food should be decreased after neutering as the metabolic rate will slow down. His coat, if long, will likely get coarser and require more maintenance. Ask your vet for advice before deciding. Keeping a dog or bitch intact requires very responsible owners who are prepared to ensure there are no unwanted litters produced.

78

Don't Chase Like A Collie
How to teach your do
to bring back a toy

Getting your dog hooked on a game with a ball, from a very young age, will foster a strong foundation for a great recall.

To teach a retrieve, simply use two balls, and when puppy comes back with one, instead of trying to take it from him, encourage him to drop it by teasing with the other ball. Most will drop the one they have for your one, especially if you add movement, i.e., bounce it. As soon as he drops his ball, throw the one you have. He will quickly learn you are a key part of the game, and you cause the game to continue, rather than ending it.

If your pup won't come back, you can use a long line to encourage him or go and sit where he brings it back to, i.e., his bed. It's important to end the game when the pup is still keen, and to put the toys away from him. These toys are special and used to bond and play with you. Don't let puppy have access to them on his own. He will chew them to pieces or get bored of them quickly. Practice outside in as many places as you can. This will teach him to look to you for fun and engagement on a walk and prevent him from wanting to chase cars, joggers, birds, etc.

Trained Puppies Don't Bite Children

79

Don't Become An Indulgent Mother
"Git" -the training steps

Boundaries and rules help children find stability and contentment in life, and the same is true for dogs. One of my top rules in my house is if they are told to GIT, they must immediately get out of my personal space. What they do after that, I don't care (within reason). I teach this simply by using body language. I usually start to teach it on a walk, when I am holding a toy, but I don't want them leaping around in front of me anticipating a throw (and annoying me). Wearing a stern expression and flicking my hand away from me I tell them GIT in a low tone. I will sometimes take out my phone too, to signal to them that I am not available to them. Or if I have a lead in my hand, I will flick that towards the dog (not to hit him but just to drive him forward).

In the home you may need to use a house line, or if you are on the couch and he is attempting to get on your lap, you may have to get up as you say GIT, so he gets displaced. It is a very useful command to give power and authority to children in the house also, so the dog learns to respect them too. If he ignored the child's command, make sure you back them up by standing beside them and repeating it. This way you show unity and partnership to your dog, keeping him at the bottom of the pecking order.

Dogs, like children need to learn that you are not always available to them, even if you are in the same room.

80

Your Allowed To Control Where Your Dog Needs To Be

"In/out" - the training steps

In/out: I teach all my dogs to go on command through doors or into crates or cars, and to be called out again if need be. This is taught simply using a thrown piece of food. Throw a treat out the back door and say, 'Oscar out'. Call him in with a treat, 'Oscar in'. He will quickly learn to go in and out whenever you ask.

Owners tell me they struggle to get their dogs to go to bed at night. These are owners who have never taught the dog what the in/ out command is, so obviously, as their dog has no prior positive experience of it, the command turns into a conflict. It may be the only time of day the dog is asked to do something, and it signals the end of his company and attention from people, so naturally he may rebel. Teaching the command has a positive outcome (all my dogs get a chewy going to bed) and taking any conflict out of it by using a house line to back it up will quickly get results.

Remember aggression breeds aggression, so if you try to intimidate your dog to move somewhere, you are likely to be met with an aggressive display, and you then risk losing that encounter. Be smarter and simply use the line to lead your dog to where you need him to be. He will quickly learn to follow your command as you simply will make it happen anyway.

81

Your Dog Shouldn't Replace Your Social Life
Adolescent chewing issues

Dogs also go through a secondary development phase in the teenage years. This varies between six and eighteen months depending on the breed. If not exercised and stimulated enough as well as being kept aware of his boundaries, he will start to re-explore his home environment. I compare it to an 18 year old who is ready and excited to leave home and go to college. He wants to meet new people, learn new skills, visit exciting places. And then you put the breaks on and refuse to let him go and insist he repeats the last year of school. Imagine the acting out and displays of frustration and stress you will encounter- not pretty. If a dog's needs aren't met they will act out in a similar manner. Dogs will use their teeth to try and reduce stress and frustration, so chairs and furnishings, he never touched when he was teething, may now become the target of his fully developed adult teeth, often with damaging consequences. In order to keep your home intact and your dog safe, you may need to go back to using a crate for a few months, or any 100% chew safe area. This means when you are out of the house or sleeping, your dog isn't able to destroy your home, and will instead chew suitable items you leave for him.

Dog toys are not intended for intense chewing for dog. They will quickly get broken and your dog could get very sick by ingesting them. Suitable long-lasting chews include reindeer and buffalo horn, yak milk chews, cow hooves, pig's ears and raw meaty bones.

Don't fall into the rabbit hole of staying with your dog all the time. We all need time away from our dogs (and children), just make sure they are safe and secure when you do it.

82

Your Bedroom Is Your Castle
Should your dog sleep in your bed?

I am a light sleeper, (who loves her sleep, and is quite demonic without it!), so having my dogs (or children) sleep in my room permanently was never going to be an option. My twin girls were moved into the adjoining room of my cottage when they were nine weeks old. And I enjoyed de babying my room. Saying that, my dogs (and children) are welcome to come in for cuddles in the mornings, especially the lazy weekend ones.

For your dog, simply keeping the door closed will stop him gaining access to it. The room is your sleeping area and smells strongly of you. A pushy young dog might see it as his right to have access to this prized throne and may even resort to guarding it.

For me, sleeping with your dog in the bed is a definite no no. There have been many instances of owners getting badly bitten when they inadvertently roll on or just pet their dog when he is fully asleep. The startled dog can easily lash out without being fully aware of what's going on. This lack of (in my view) responsible dog ownership inevitably leads to the dog losing his life. So, do him a favour and get a teddy (or a man) instead.

83

Beware Of The 'Barkclash'
How to teach a quiet command

Unwanted barking in the home can be stressful on both the dog and
the owner and can lead to potential issues with neighbours. Ironically
teaching your dog to be quiet involves firstly teaching your dog to
bark on command. For an upcoming dog show I need to teach my
dog Cassie to bark five times on command. So I needed to find a way
to get her to bark so I could reward that behaviour and then put it on
command. She is an excellent guard dog and when someone rings the
doorbell she will bark enthusiastically. I started the training with my
daughter outside ringing the doorbell and I simply sat with Cassie, in
the living room verbally praising her and giving her a treat any time
she barked. On our second training session I controlled the doorbell
at the front door and again simply rewarded her when she barked.
Next I needed to replace the sound of the doorbell with my SPEAK
command so before I rang the bell I issued my SPEAK command and
I continued to reward all barking. After a few repetitions I was able
to remove the sound of the doorbell and use my SPEAK command
to prompt the barking. Now that I could verbally command her to
SPEAK I faded rewarding the speak and waited for a few seconds
of silence. I now started to reward the silence and soon added
the QUIET command. Pretty soon I was able to issue my QUIET
command in a realistic scenario when she was barking at a cat out

the window. I would class the QUIET command as an instructional reprimand which simultaneously interrupts unwanted behaviour whilst educating the dog on what you do want them to do thus giving you a chance to reward good behaviour.

84

Pretend To Agree
The importance of unity in the household

Consistency is key in any relationship, and this is all the more important in the dog/human relationship. If there are two adults (this includes children in the dog's world) in the home, it is hugely important that both are consistent in implementing rules and boundaries for your dog. Any weakness in this show of power and togetherness will potentially mean your dog will act differently with each human. Usually, but not always, this means they will respect the authority of the man but may exploit perceived weakness or inconsistency in the woman or children in the household. I see this in training classes, where there is sometimes a vast difference in behaviour of the dog, depending on who is handling him. Ensure you back up any commands given by anyone more vulnerable in the home and show unity and support to each other. This is especially important with the larger more dominant breeds.

85

Don't Aim For Absolute Equality
Allow ranks to develop within the dog family

With our children we go above and beyond to make them feel loved and treasured equally. When we anthropomorphise our dogs and try to do the same we often run into problems. Dogs don't want to exist in a society where all are created equal. This breeds too much conflict. They thrive on a hierarchy structure, where each knows their position and doesn't feel threatened by those below him or victimised by those above. If you have dog to dog issues in the home, these usually arise when the owner is around and is upsetting the apple cart. Left to their own devices they will naturally (usually) have a higher and lower rank. The higher-ranking dog should receive recognition from the owner for the rank he has. He should be fed first, get the lead on first, allowed up on the couch first (if you allow it), and be backed up during minor skirmishes with lower ranking dogs. Our human nature inevitably gets in the way, and we want to comfort and support the underdog. A better understanding of the dog's needs will, however, result in a calmer happier household for all. This is especially true for the underdog, as he will not be subjected to attacks from the more dominant dog, as he tries to redress the balance that the human has undone. Remember my example of Meggie and Cassie.

86

Dogs Are
A Separate Species
Poo eating dogs

Poo eating! A disgusting habit that very quickly will remind us that our cute little 'fur baby' is in fact a totally different species. It is a common habit among puppies, as they bid to explore their new world with their mouths. If it progresses into adulthood, there are several possible reasons and solutions.

Quality of dog food: The dog food might not be easily absorbed by the gut resulting in the poo being more appetising than it is designed to be. The solution for this is to switch to a higher quality, easier to absorb food.

Learned behaviour: Puppies punished for pooing indoors, or who (God forbid) have their nosed rubbed in it, may decide to hide the evidence to avoid a scolding. The solution to this is not to punish the pup, especially if it's after the event. Be more diligent and reward all pooing outside. Interrupt verbally and with alarmed body language if caught in the act but never inflict pain or threaten violence.

Boredom: A dog left outdoors alone for long periods may develop the habit, either with his own poo and other dogs' poo. The solution to this if boredom is causing him to eat his own poo is to advise responsible rehoming to more committed owners. Management, i.e., regular picking up of poo, and training a solid LEAVE IT command will help stop this habit.

87

Praise Your Dog For The Mastery Of The Mundane
"Leave It"- the training steps

Seeing your puppy strut masterfully around with his favourite teddy might seem like a boring regular occurrence, but by giving good verbal encouragement 'what a clever strong puppy you are', will encourage him to choose his own toys to play with, and not your handbag. It's very easy to get bogged down by the unwanted behaviour your dog is exhibiting and how you can 'fix' it. Equally, (and even more importantly) you should actively reward through verbal praise, touch, food, and toys, behaviour you do like. Remember that what is rewarded gets repeated, and if he is doing something you approve off, he's not getting up to mischief. Dogs, especially gundogs, are driven to explore the world with their mouths and use them like hands. Providing them with an acceptable outlet for this will keep him out of a lot of trouble. A 'Leave It' command is a very useful exercise to teach, so you can reward him for doing what you ask rather than trying to punish him for wrecking your new shoes. How to teach a Leave it command

1. When you have your dog's attention, place a treat under your foot.

2. Wait while your dog tries his best to get the treat out. Be patient and say nothing.

3. Eventually he will pause and look away.

4. Immediately mark this behaviour with clicker (if using one) or marker word, e.g., "YES" and reward with the exact same type of treat from your hand.

5. Repeat this several times. You may have to lift your foot occasionally to show him the treat and keep his interest.

6. After a few repetitions he should become quicker at not trying to get the treat under your foot and should back away and look to you.

7. Continue to mark and reward from your hand.

8. Remember to smile, praise, and pet before giving the treat.

9. After a few sessions, when he is backing away immediately at the start of the exercise you can start to introduce your word of command "leave it". Use a distinctive and consistent tone.

10. Graduate to lifting your foot off the treat and telling your dog to "leave it". If he does reward lavishly. If not cover the treat again quickly and go back a few steps.

11. Build up to leaving a treat on a table or chair or leaving distractions like food or toys out in your garden.

12. When you start using the command out and about keep your dog on a long line until the training is established so you can continue to train successfully.

13. Keep the value of the reward high, especially for really good "leave its". Use jackpot rewards like multiple treats and excitable praise along with high energy games.

88

Maintain Some Fun In Your Walk
A tale of two collies
– when chase instinct emerges

I was on a walk with my dogs recently where I met two separate owners with almost identical black and white border collies. Both dogs were exhibiting typical collie type like behaviour but while one dog was very likely to stay in its home and enjoy wonderful off lead walks for the rest of his life, the other dog was most likely going to get into serious trouble. The first dog walker, a female, I witnessed from about the distance of a football field. Her dog was racing off ahead of her and to the untrained eye it might have looked like she had little control. But around 20 metres out, he circled crouched into a down and stared intently at his owner. His owner obliged by picking up a stick and throwing it towards the dog. The dog pounced forward to catch the stick, played with it for a few seconds and then repeated his run-out. Although I would have preferred to see the dog playing with a toy rather than a stick, at least this owner understood that engaging with her dog on some level was going to keep him nearby, safe and under control.

The second owner, a male, I witnessed with his dog off-lead, at a distance of about half a football field. He managed to encourage his dog to stay with him while he passed me and my dogs approaching from some bushes but thereafter lost interest in his dog and walked for several meters without turning to see what he was doing. I opted to go in a different direction with my dogs but a walker without a dog followed in the direction of this dog owner. This prompted the border collie to repeat the behaviour of the other collie but his target was not a stick but the approaching single walker. He went down into a crouch and stared intently at the approaching woman. I watched this unfolding with a sense of horror but luckily in this case the dog realized that its owner had gotten very far away and opted to turn and catch up with him. I'm guessing that dog owner has very little knowledge of the ticking time bomb going off in his dog. It is only a matter of time before he stalks the wrong person or builds up the confidence to bark or even nip at an approaching pedestrian.

Both collies were exhibiting very natural behaviour specific to their genetic traits. One owner was allowing her dog to carry out this natural behaviour in a controlled manner and unfortunately the second dog owner was not which could ultimately lead him to losing his pet home or worse his life.

89

Eating Should Be Dog Time
Food guarding issues

Some pet owners believe in order to avoid food guarding they should regularly put their hand in the dog's food or even take it away completely. When you really sit down and think rationally about this, how can it even make sense? Would you feel more trust and confidence around someone who randomly took your dinner or stuck their hands in your mashed potato? Or would you start to defend it?

I have a rule in my house not to ever take food off a dog or bother them when they are eating. This is so important around young children also. A dog should never feel threatened around his food bowl. Serious food aggression can even develop into the dog guarding his empty bowl, or the press where the food is kept. In most cases food aggression in puppies starts with the breeder. An insufficient amount of food bowls and sometimes even food, will lead to fighting and squabbling which will carry though into the home with the owners, especially if they keep bothering him.

Signs of mild food aggression can be puppy freezing or eating faster when you approach. Low growling while eating may be heard too. This can usually be rectified by dropping, from a distance, a higher value food in every time you pass. Puppy will build an association that people approaching their food bowl equals extra tasty food arriving. Over time this should replace the unease and insecurity he feels.

More serious guarding, such as showing teeth, air snapping, lunging, and biting should be addressed by a trained professional. It should be addressed as swiftly as possible to avoid bad habits forming and the guarding to potentially extend to other items and locations. A good "leave it" command will enable you to safely ask your dog to move away from food without conflict.

90

No Negotiation On The Table
The security, finality and beauty of the word NO

In her book Druckerman references Jean-Jacques Rousseau's contention, made 250 years ago, that perpetual negotiations are bad for children. 'The worst education is to leave him floating between his will and yours, and to dispute endlessly between you and him as to which of the two will be master'. This statement is as true for the dog/owner relationship as it is for the child/parent relationship. This tedious tug of war existence for a dog is stressful and unsettling. I have encountered many dogs, who in their owner's arms are barking, neurotic messes, and who instantly transform into docile obedient and most importantly relaxed dogs once they are enthused to my care. The solace of having a relationship with someone, me, with clear boundaries and kind, fair handling takes a huge weight off their shoulders. The guessing game of what their owner will and will not allow at any given time is blissfully over. Inevitably they turn back into the neurotic messes they once were when they hear the owner's car pull up, and so back to their lives with inconsistent rules, badly timed rewards and sometimes ineffectual punishing. Druckerman states 'if the parent isn't there to stop him, then he's the one who's going to have to stop himself, or not stop himself, and that's much more anxiety provoking'

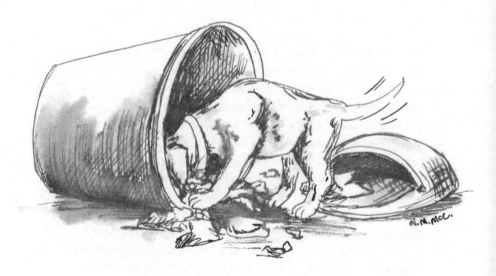

91

Say NO With Conviction
Negative punishment explained

Negative punishment involves removing something from the dog in order to try and decrease the probability of a behaviour being repeated. In my training classes I use negative punishment on the last night to help with recall issues. This is only after owners have spent six weeks diligently training a recall command in different scenarios and using a multiple of rewards. If, in the hall, the dog then chooses to ignore the recall command in favour of smelling the ground or approaching other dogs and people I will use a long line to encourage the dog to make a good decision and go back to their owner. However I will then instruct the owner to show the dog the rewards that they would have gotten had they complied and to put these rewards back in their pocket. I will then remove the dog again a short distance and ask the owner to call them. In most cases the dog is now extremely keen to get back to the owner. The removal of the reward decreased the dog's desire to ignore the dog owner's command. In multi dog households, I tell owners they can give rewards to other dogs in the household, put them in the bin or even eat them themselves to reinforce to the dog the consequence of their actions.

92

Punish Rarely
But Make It Count
The similarities are clear

There are so many lines in "French Parents don't Give In", that really sum up to me how similar the French way of parenting is similar to my own way of raising both my children and dogs! Here are some:

Punishment is 'a big deal, it's not something that happens every night at dinner'.

'Punishment should be administered immediately and matter-of-factly, without malice.'

Parents are 'careful to warn children before punishing them'.

'Parents typically send a young child to her room to 'marinate' or think on it.

'For older children, the punishment is often a few days without TV, computers or video games.'

'After a conflict, it's the parent's role to re-establish the connection between the two of them again, for example the suggestion that they play a favourite game together.'

The similarities are startling to me, and to you too now I hope!

Giving fair warnings, using evictions and removing cherished items all work effectively as negative consequences on both children and puppies.

The major difference between using a negative consequence with kids and dogs, is that you can explain to a child the future consequences of their actions. You cannot do this with a dog. Any consequence, good or bad, must come within 2 seconds of the behaviour you wish to affect. They don't 'know' they have done something wrong if you 'challenge' them after the event is over. If they look guilty, they are simply reacting to your foul mood and aggressive body language, trying to pacify you.

They actually have no idea why you are angry. They just don't have the cognitive ability to connect the dots.

But more importantly, with both species, is the education on how you DO wish them to behave, and the development of a strong bond through mutual respect and play.

93

Explain the reason behind the "D" The 5 D's

Once you start to train a command you need to incorporate the 3 D's. Using STAY as an example, these are as follows:

Distraction: adding the presence of another dog to the STAY exercise

Duration: working on longer periods of STAY

Distance: asking for a STAY when your dog is further away from you

I like to add 2 more D's to this, so owners can get a fuller picture of the real-life training process

Destination: Dogs are situational learners and initially will associate the training environment with the command. If you imagine the dog has a camera in his paws and takes a picture the second you tell him to STAY. From the dog's point of view, everything in the picture is responsible for communicating to him the need the STAY. When you take him out of that context, to the local park, for example, he will probably look confused or totally ignore you when you ask him to stay, as this picture is now different from the first one, he took. This is especially true if you just expect to pick up as your left off on your last training session at home. It is not a failure to go back a few steps, in a new environment, to make it easier for the dog to succeed and then over time to generalise and recognise that STAY means STAY, even on the moon!

Disinclination: What to do if despite your training efforts and doing all of the above and working on your dog's motivation, your dog decides to ignore you. Here are a few options!

1. Honestly assess your dog's living environment to ensure he's not getting rewarded by behaviour you ultimately want to discourage.

2. Look at your rewards and ensure your dog doesn't have free access to the toys or food you are using.

3. Use body language to back up your vocal commands to help your dog understand.

4. Repeat a command only once using a clearer tone or change to a previously taught command such as LEAVE IT or QUIET, if the situation warrants it.

5. Use your lead or long line to direct your dog's focus back to you, and /or create distance from any distractions.

6. Lower your requirements to set your dog up for success.

7. Remove rewards – let your dog see you put them in a bin or back in your pocket or eat them!

8. Give an emotional response to your dogs' lack of focus– remember shocked and disappointed rather than scary!

Only by being aware of and utilizing all of the 5 D's will you get a dog who fully understands all of your commands in every scenario.

94

Sometimes your dog will jump
How to inhibit jumping up

Jumping up on people is a problem most dog owners face. From a puppy's point of view it is a natural social ritual as they try and show submission by licking an elder's face. As pet owners we often encourage and allow this behaviour when the puppies are small and cute. It is only when they grow, and the novelty wanes a little that the issue becomes apparent. There are several approaches to try and inhibit this behaviour.

Most jumping up is an attention seeking behaviour. Attention for a dog is eye contact, touch and being spoken to, so if you want to decrease the likelihood of this behaviour continuing you would take away those rewards. So, when your dog jumps up you would fold your arms, turn around and just give a negative 'Ah Ah' tone to communicate your displeasure.

As you will know by now, stopping behaviour on its own is never an answer. Educating the dog on how you do want them to behave is vital to long-term success. Therefore you must work extra hard to teach your dog a 'sit' and reward them lavishly when they comply. Hold him gently by the collar as he's sitting to discourage any forward movement and do the same when he is greeting other people.

If your dog is particularly strong and is jumping on strangers on a walk you could try standing on the lead, so he is comfortable in a standing or sitting position but is prevented from moving forward. Alternatively, you can link the lead through a solid object such as a gate if there is one nearby

Scattering food treats on the ground when you arrive home or when there are guests in the house will further reinforce to the dog that all four feet on the ground is positively rewarding for them.

95

De-dramatize
Pain not aggression

Many behaviour issues such as growling snapping and biting can be caused by pain within the dog. Dogs cannot ask us to bring them to a vet when they're feeling poorly and we as owners are often ill equipped to interpret this pain. Humans get grumpy, touch sensitive, and reclusive when in pain and dogs will often do the same. When we or other dogs intrude on their personal space while they are feeling pain aggressive outbursts can occur.

I often recount a story told to me by renowned dog expert John Rogerson almost 18 years ago. He had a client with a beautiful German shepherd dog that out of the blue bit the family's young child. The owners were devastated but felt the only option opened to them was to have the dog put to sleep. The vet was upset at having to put down such a beautiful dog with no track record of aggression and asked the owners if he could perform an autopsy to try and find the root cause of the outburst. He suspected maybe an undiagnosed cancer or perhaps a brain tumour. Imagine his horror and surprise when he found a 3 inch sharpened pencil jammed in the dogs ear canal. The owners failed to properly supervise their young child with their dog which resulted in putting their dog in an impossible position where he had to defend himself from a little child he most likely loved. I always hope this story will stick with anyone I tell it to and may potentially save another beautiful family pet from a one way visit to the vet.

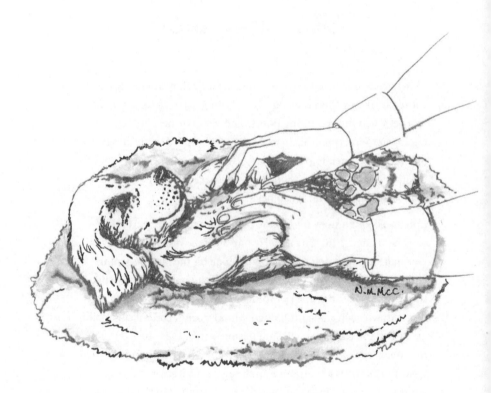

96

You're Not Disciplining, You're Educating
Extinction and the earthquake effect

Extinction is a training tool that can be useful when dealing with attention seeking behaviour. For example a dog that cries, scratches and whines in a crate. In essence extinction means ignoring the behaviour until it eventually fades away and disappears. All behaviour has a reinforcer i.e., there is something in it for the dog. In order for extinction to work you must have control over that reinforcer. It is equally important to recognise and reward incompatible and desired behaviour such as calm relaxed behaviour in the crate. When using extinction for attention seeking behaviour you must recognize that for a dog attention is looking at them, touching them and talking to them so all these reinforcers must be stopped while you were trying to decrease the attention seeking behaviour. Ideally you want to wait for two minutes of quiet, calm behaviour which you can then reward. I like to reward quiet behaviour in a crate from a pot of treats on top of the crate and dropped from above. You must be wary of the extinction burst. This occurs after an initial increase in the dog's better behaviour. There will be a sudden eruption where the behaviour is worse, possibly even worse than it was originally.

It's very important not to give in as this too will pass and the gradual improvement will return until the behaviour is truly extinct.

If for whatever reason you cannot use extinction for this problem I will use what I call the earthquake effect. This is a type of 'Interrupter' I will use for a crated dog that is whining scratching or barking. I of course make sure that all the dog's needs are met before he or she is placed in the crate and that the time has been taken to teach the dog that the crate is a safe place to be. Attention seeking barking in crates will sometimes erupt during adolescence even in dogs that have previously been calm and well behaved in crates. When the dog is in the crate I will cover it with a thick blanket with only the front uncovered. Depending on the scenario I will disappear behind the dog's crate or have an accomplice help. The very second the attention seeking behaviour starts I or my accomplice will deliver a swift kick to the back of the crate. The blanket will prevent the dog from seeing that a human has caused this earthquake under its body and it should only take two or three repetitions to inhibit and interrupt the attention seeking. You now have an opportunity to get two minutes of quiet and reward that behaviour.

97

Make the Big eyes
Using humane consequences

The subject of punishment is a tricky topic in dog training circles currently. There is a growing trend towards force-free training, stemming from an overabundance of publicity for more forceful types of trainers. You will know by now that I wholeheartedly disagree with using harsh punishments such as choking, pinching or electrocuting your dogs in order to get them to comply. This is an absolute no brainer for me. And with my formal training for obedience and agility I am 100% positive and force-free. I rarely even use a lead.

But if you live in a home with your dog, common sense dictates that there are times when you need to communicate to your dog that he needs to stop doing whatever he is doing, for his safety or the safety of others. And, I worry, if the average dog owner isn't educated on how to do this in a humane manner they may very well resort to more punitive means. To sum up, these are the negative consequences or interrupters I will occasionally use on dogs if the situation warrants it.

Please note: Always be aware of the reaction of the dog in front of you. I own one extremely sensitive dog where if I even blow on my nails she gets extremely upset. Only use the minimum amount of interruption needed in order to stop the dog in his tracks and immediately educate him on how you do want him to behave and reward – Interrupt, Redirect, Reward (I.R.R)

1. I will use 'Ah Ah' in a low, disapproving tone.

2. I will use 'Ah Ah' in a low, disapproving tone and lead my dog to another area of the house for two minutes-eviction.

3. I will use an instructive reprimand which I have already taught such as 'leave it', 'drop' or 'quiet' depending on the scenario.

4. I will use 'Ah Ah' in a low, disapproving tone, and approach my dog quickly stamping my feet and clapping my hands.

5. I will use a unique sound or motion to interrupt.

Remember your dog should never be afraid to 'make up' with you after you have interrupted him. Many unwanted behaviours stem from lack of training, lack of good quality off-lead exercise, lack of edible chewing items, lack of management and lack of opportunities to carry out natural behaviour.

Don't forget, you must make every effort to give him an alternative, acceptable behaviour to enjoy so you can both continue to enjoy your lives together in harmony.

Both children and dogs benefit far more from being told how they should behave rather than being constantly told what they shouldn't be doing.

98

Give Dogs Time To Comply
Why using harsh punishment can backfire

Harsh punishment methods have in my view no place in dog training. I am particularly adverse to the use of electric shock collars. I've inadvertently witnessed first-hand how terrifying they can be for a dog and how easily the dogs can misinterpret their intended use. I live in the countryside and unfortunately electric fences are something my dogs eventually experience. About four years ago I was walking with my three dogs and my 4-year-old twin girls down a country lane. There was a small stream running alongside the lane and the girls had stopped to throw some pebbles into the water. I was throwing the ball into an adjoining field on realizing the electric fence was on. While coming back with a thrown ball I heard a yelp and poor Tilly dropped the ball and ran to hide under my legs. I immediately knew what had happened and I consoled her and we moved on from that area pretty quickly afterwards. A week later we went on the same walk and at approximately 200 meters from the spot where she got electrocuted, Tilly started exhibiting fearful behaviour - her tail was down, her head was down, she was trying to hide beneath my legs and she made a couple of attempts to run back to the car. I avoided this walk for a few weeks hoping that the memory would fade. However, the behaviour occurred again on two different walks where she had never experienced electrocution. To my consternation and without any explanation she became fearful, she desired to be close to me, she refused to play and she shook with fear. I was totally perplexed and quite frankly a bit frustrated by her behaviour. I needed to put my thinking cap on. It is one of the most interesting and also frustrating things about working with dog behaviour- you are essentially a detective trying to dig beneath the layers of a dog's feelings and emotions to uncover the root cause for a behaviour. For this is where you must start if you want true behaviour change to occur. After a few sleepless nights I had a light-bulb moment. When Tilly received the original electric shock she obviously linked and associated that shock with an event which was occurring simultaneously. On reflection in all three locations my twin girls were throwing stones into water. Tilly had linked the ZAP of the electric fence with the action of my girls throwing stones into water nearby. Now that I understand the reasoning for her behaviour it was much easier to manage and understand it and it gradually decreased as her confidence grew again. But this experience really highlighted to me how in the wrong hands or even potentially experienced hands the random ZAP of pain on a dog's neck can be linked with any manner of events, people or things that may be in the dog's orbit at that split second in time. I hope in time Ireland will follow the UK's lead in banning these devices for use with pet dogs for they have no place around the necks of our best friends.

99

Say Yes As Often As You Can
Freedom of choice
makes for a happier dog

I sincerely hope that this book reaches people at the very start of their journey to becoming a dog owner. I hope it inspires people to say YES to researching your breed, to say YES to researching your breeder or rescue, to say YES to considering your puppies needs and desires throughout his whole life, and not just your needs. I have a 16-year-old dog, Meggie, who is now unreliable with her bladder, mostly deaf and blind, and barks constantly in the car unless she is beside me in the front seat. I have had to make adjustments and sacrifices in my life to accommodate that, but I gladly do it for all the joy she has given me in my life.

I was lucky enough to have the proper advice when I chose her. She came from a farm where I knew her mother and grandmother and could vouch for their temperament and health. The conditions for the bitch and litter were good and I got to take her home at 6 weeks of age.

By prioritising health and temperament, and getting a breed that suited my lifestyle, I got the perfect family pet dog who is rarely sick and is a dream in all scenarios.

I ran a rescue for 8 years and often visited the local high-kill pound. I often had to look into the eyes of young healthy puppies, knowing they were soon to die. They may have committed the cardinal sin of knocking over a child or chasing a chicken-normal puppy behaviour but in the minds of some inexperienced or misinformed owners, enough to warrant a one-way ticket to the pound.

I believe every potential dog owner should have to visit a pound first and learn the stories of each dog and puppy there. Only by learning from the sins of the past can we hope for a brighter future for the pet dogs of Ireland.

Trained Puppies Don't Bite Children

100

Sometimes there's a Twist in the Tale
A Visit to France

I had a different chapter written for a final 'au revoir' of this book. But a chance visit to France two weeks ago has prompted me to write a different ending. I knew from the French parenting book of the view that French children were somehow better behaved than Anglican children. It was my recognition of the similarity of their no-nonsense child rearing skills to my dog rearing skills, that prompted me to write this book. But it never occurred to me to wonder if 'French puppies don't throw food' either. I visited the beautiful port town of la Rochelle for five days. It is my guess that I witnessed over 100 dogs during this period, of all shapes and sizes. I was blown away by how well mannered, calm and fit these dogs were. Most were on lead, but many were not. Most dogs ignored other dogs or had a cursory sniff. Is it because French dogs are allowed more places and are therefore more relaxed in public? Is it because a quick Google search revealed the presence of very little doggie daycares in France? Is it because a lot of French businesses close in the afternoon meaning owners spend more time with their dogs? Is it because they have a no-nonsense approach to dog rearing also? I don't know the answer to these questions but I do know there was a stark difference in the behaviour and the weight of these French dogs compared to most Irish dogs I meet. Maybe as a trainer I am biased as I often see more badly behaved dogs then well-adjusted dogs. Or maybe the French have figured out how to have beautifully behaved and well adjusted dogs too? Has their child-rearing ethos filtered through to how they rear puppies? I fear these questions might warrant a closer inspection and study of the dogs in France and a follow up book which may provide some answers. I might just have to oblige. Bonjour Paris.

Reference

Druckerman, P. (2013), French Parents Don't Give In, London, Transworld Publishers.

Recommended websites:

Dogsfirst.ie

Allaboutdogfood.co.uk

Johnrogerson.com

Drdogcare.ie

Pameladruckerman.com